Basics
of
Biblical
Praying

Basics
of
Biblical
Praying

A Primer on Prayer

by
Frank R. Shivers

Unless otherwise noted, Scripture quotations are from
The Holy Bible *King James Version*

Library of Congress Cataloging-in-Publication Data

Shivers, Frank R., 1949-
Basics of Biblical Praying / Frank Shivers
ISBN 978-1-878127-49-5

Library of Congress Control Number:
2022913205

Cover design by
Tim King

For Information:
Frank Shivers Evangelistic Association
P. O. Box 9991
Columbia, South Carolina 29290
www.frankshivers.com

PRESENTED TO

_____

BY

_____

DATE

_____

Publications by Frank R. Shivers
"We are not writing upon water but carving upon imperishable material."[1] ~ C. H. Spurgeon

The Widow's Comfort
When Things Just Don't Make Sense
When the Rain Comes
The Treasure of Grace
Persecuted for Christ's Sake
Basics of Biblical Praying
Christian Basics 101
Grief Beyond Measure, But Not Beyond Grace
Grief Beyond Measure, But Not Beyond Grace (Funeral Home Version)
Growing Old, Honorably and Happily
The Wounded Spirit
The Wounded Spirit: Companion Workbook
Growing in Knowledge, Living by Faith
Marriage and Parenting Boosters
Caught Up to Heaven
Expositions of the Psalms (Three Volumes)
Life Principles from Proverbs
The Evangelism Apologetic Study Bible
Hot Buttons on Apologetics
Hot Buttons on Morality
Hot Buttons on Discipleship
The Pornography Trap
The Poison of Porn
Heavy Stuff
Heavy Stuff (Student Workbook)
Clear Talk to Students
Nuggets of Truth (Three Volumes)
Soulwinning 101
Spurs to Soulwinning
Evangelistic Preaching 101
Evangelistic Praying

The Evangelistic Invitation 101
The Minister and the Funeral
Revivals 101
Children's Sermons That Connect
Be Careful Little Eyes
How to Preach Without Evangelistic Results (Pamphlet)
False Hopes of Heaven (Tract)
First Steps for New Believers (Tract)
The Goal Line Stand (Tract)
The Death Clock (Tract)

"We cannot all argue, but we can all pray; we cannot all be leaders, but we can all be pleaders; we cannot all be mighty in rhetoric, but we can all be prevalent in prayer."[2] ~ C. H. Spurgeon

To

Dr. Eldon Sloan

With gratitude for his abiding friendship and unfailing support of my ministry.

"We ought to pray for the desire to pray; for such a desire is God-given and heaven-born."[3] ~ E. M. Bounds

Contents

Preface

Basics of Biblical Praying is an instructional and inspirational book on the ABCs of prayer that is simple enough for the new believer to understand, yet deep enough to enhance the prayer life of the oldest saint. Included are biblical insights from E. M. Bounds, Andrew Murray, Samuel Chadwick, C. H. Spurgeon, J. C. Ryle, John Bunyan, S. D. Gordon, D. L. Moody, A. W. Pink, Ole Hallesby, Gordon B. Watt, John Wesley, D. A. Carson, John MacArthur, John R. Rice, Matthew Henry, and Oswald Chambers.

J. C. Ryle said, "Whatever throws light on the subject of prayer is for our soul's health."[4] May the Holy Spirit be pleased to use that which is cited in the following pages to add illumination to the work and efficacy of prayer and prompt you to engage in it more fervently and consistently in your life (as has been the case with myself in writing it).

> There is a bridge, whereof the span
> Is rooted in the heart of man
> And reaches, without pile or rod,
> Unto the Great White Throne of God.
> Its traffic is in human sighs
> Fervently wafted to the skies.
> 'Tis the one pathway from despair,
> And it is called the Bridge of Prayer. ~ Gilbert Thomas

"Prayer pulls the rope below, and the great bell rings above in the ears of God. Some scarcely stir the bell, for they pray so languidly. Others give but an occasional pluck at the rope. But he who wins with Heaven is the man who grasps the rope boldly and pulls continuously, with all his might."[5] ~ C.H. Spurgeon

PART ONE
Basics of Prayer

Chapter 1
Christ's School of Prayer

"Jesus has opened a school in which He trains His redeemed ones who specially desire it to have power in prayer. Shall we not enter it with the petition: 'Lord! It is just this we need to be taught! Oh, teach us to pray.'"[6] ~ Andrew Murray

Christ's school of prayer maintains open enrollment. Its admission requirement is based on the new birth and desire to learn how to pray. Attendance is voluntary and tuition is free. Its curriculum consists solely of intercession and prayer. Its Principal and Teacher is Christ, an Instructor eminently qualified; and His Helper is the Holy Spirit. Its course is arduous and laden with discipline, difficulty, discouragement, and distraction.

Its textbook is the Holy Scriptures—the model prayer of Jesus, the law of asking and receiving, the certainty of the promise and power of prayer, the Psalter. Its classroom is the closet, an inner chamber shut out from the world. Its classes are never cancelled, and there are no holidays or summer breaks or interruptions due to teacher absenteeism. Its homework is in daily prayer.

The instruction is personal, one to one. The grading scale is based on grace—none ever fail. Its term is for a lifetime; from this school none graduate. Its truancy rate is high; multitudes are not skilled petitioners because they ceased to attend. Achievement is not measured by academics, but by spiritual, intimate fellowship with Christ and participation in His kingdom work around the world.

Its inaugural class included twelve ordinary men that said, "Lord, teach us to pray." Prayer was not something that came naturally to them (nor does it to any man); they needed divine instruction to learn it and become proficient in it. Never is it recorded that they asked to be taught how to witness, heal, or preach. But they did see the overwhelming need for Christ to teach them the essentials of prayer. Just that in itself speaks of prayer's utmost and vital importance.

All it takes to attend Christ's school of prayer is to join the disciples in saying, "Lord, teach us to pray" (Luke 11:1).

Blessed Savior, we acknowledge our frailty in prayer. It is often limp, impotent, weak, cold, formal, heartless, and based upon unscriptural principles. Thank You for providing the school of prayer and being its Superintendent and Teacher, that we might learn how to pray powerfully, proficiently, and expectantly while communing with You intimately. Draw us often to its classroom—our closet, that secret place—to unload burdens; confess sin; gain strength, comfort, and courage; receive guidance; intercede for others; do battle with the powers of darkness; and request provision and power for Thy kingdom work and its workers. Thank You for the promise to meet us in that sacred spot to teach us how to pray, to supply our need, and to give answer to that which we ask. Teach us to remain steadfast in the school of prayer until ushered into Thy holy presence in Heaven. In Thy name, Amen.

Chapter 2

What Prayer Is and Is Not

"Prayer is God's appointed means for appropriating the blessings that are ours in Christ Jesus."[7] ~ D. A. Carson

Prayer is not a religious duty. Prayer is not a means to gain God's approval. Prayer is not getting God to change His mind.

Prayer is not the formalistic recitation of a petition. Prayer is not telling God what to do (prayer, although directed *to* God, "is not to be directing God"[8]). Prayer is not, as Luther says, "overcoming God's reluctance, but laying hold of God's willingness."[9] Prayer is not a ritualistic habit void of thought, piety, or earnestness. Prayer is not grandstanding before others (to impress others with your devotion). Prayer is not "some mystical process whereby we call out to some force."[10] Prayer is not informing God of anything. Prayer is not a sermon clothed in its garb. Prayer is not a vending machine or candy dispenser. "Prayer is not wrestling with God's reluctance to bless us," says John Blanchard; "it is laying hold on His willingness to do so."[11]

What is prayer? Whereas no text in Scripture defines prayer *per se,* the consensus of the Word of God is that it is a two-way conversation or dialog with God (Exodus 34:29). The best of man's definitions of prayer is like defining a majestic mountain, exquisite waterfall, or beautiful sunrise. It invariably falls short. But some ardently try. Spurgeon said, "Prayer is to ask of God."[12] E. W. Kenyon says, "Prayer is the voice of faith to the Father."[13]

What is prayer? Writers of the Westminster Shorter Catechism say, "Prayer is an offering up of our desires unto God for things agreeable to His will, in the name of Christ, with confession of our sins and thankful acknowledgment of His mercies."[14] John R. Rice provides this definition of prayer: "Prayer is asking God for something. Prayer is always asking."[15] Charles Hodge defines prayer: "Prayer is the converse of the soul with God. Therein we manifest or express to Him our reverence, and love for His divine perfection, our gratitude for all His mercies, our penitence (sorrow, repentance) for our sins, our hope in His forgiving love, our submission to His authority, our confidence in His care, our desires for His favor, and for the providential and spiritual blessings needed for ourselves and others."[16]

What is prayer? A. B. Simpson says, "Prayer is the link that connects us with God. It is the bridge that spans every gulf and bears us over every abyss of danger or need."[17] Charles Stanley states, "Prayer is the choice tool God has given us to reach Him, speak to Him, plead our case before Him, and receive all we need from Him."[18] Saith Francis Dixon, "Prayer does not make God more willing to give, but it provides the channel through which He can give."[19]

What is prayer? It is "a weapon [of power], based on the victory of Calvary, to bring down every stronghold of evil, to resist and overcome forces of antagonism, and to do something for God."[20]

What is prayer? It is God authorized. It is the Christian's delight and duty. It is profitable. It is governed by certain laws or conditions. It is something learned by the doing. It is without substitute. It is founded and fueled in faith. It is spiritual work. It is the precursor to any form of ministry service. It is the means of acquiring divine help in time of need. It is powerful. It is God's ordained means to accomplish His work in and through man and His kingdom on earth.

What is prayer? Samuel Chadwick states it is a paradox. "It is so simple that a child can pray, and it is so profound that the wisest cannot explain its mystery. It is so easy that those who have no strength can pray, and it is so strenuous that it taxes every resource of energy, intelligence, and power. It is so natural that it need not be taught, and it is so far beyond nature that it cannot be learned in the school of this world's wisdom. Prayer is a world in itself, and no one aspect of life's similes can explain it."[21]

Despite man's best attempt to define prayer (it but touches the hem of its celestial garment), it remains a mystery. Saith L. Nelson Bell, "Prayer is a super-natural phenomenon, a direct communication between man and God, and must be approached as such."[22] Oswald Chambers states, "Prayer is not logical; it is a mysterious moral working of the Holy Spirit."[23] It is not explainable or understandable, but it is believable through the lenses of faith and its efficacy. Understanding how prayer works is not essential to its effectiveness. Edison wrote in 1921: "We don't know the millionth part of one per cent about anything. We don't know what water is. We don't know what light is. We don't know what gravitation is. We don't know what enables us to keep on our feet when we stand up. We don't know what electricity is. We don't know what heat is. We don't know anything about magnetism. We have a lot of hypotheses about these things, but that is all. But we do not let our ignorance about all these things deprive us of their use." Inability to comprehend the spiritual mechanics of prayer mustn't deter us from using it. It's in the use of prayer that its efficacy is proven.

> Say, what is prayer, when it is prayer indeed?
> The mighty utterance of a mighty need.
> The man is praying who doth press with might
> Out of his darkness into God's own light.[24]
> ~ Richard Chenevix Trench (1807–1886)

So, what is prayer? Saith Chrysostom, "Prayer is a haven to the shipwrecked man, an anchor to them that are sinking in the waves, a staff to the limbs that totter, a mine of jewels to the poor, a healer of diseases, and a guardian of health. Prayer at once secures the continuance of our blessings and dissipates the clouds of our calamities. O blessed prayer! thou art the unwearied conqueror of human woes, the firm foundation of human happiness, the source of ever enduring joy, the mother of philosophy. The man who can pray truly, though languishing in extremest indigence, is richer than all beside; whilst the wretch who never bowed the knee, though proudly sitting as monarch of all nations, is of all men most destitute."[25]

Chapter 3

The Royal Invitation

"If we want to see mighty wonders of divine power and grace wrought in the place of weakness, failure and disappointment, let us answer God's standing challenge: 'Call unto me, and I will answer thee, and shew thee great and mighty things, which thou knowest not.'"[26] ~ J. Hudson Taylor

Subjects had restricted access to kings in biblical days. Recall that Queen Esther, for example, was denied access to King Ahasuerus unless she had been summoned. "But it is not so with us! The path to the Throne of Grace is always open—there are no guards to bar the way of those who come in the right spirit. Whenever the Spirit of God inclines the heart to pray, the ear of God is open to hear our supplications—and the mouth of God is open to grant us gracious answers of peace!"[27] See Hebrews 4:16.

A. C. Dixon states, "A throne means power. Back of it stand the army and navy ready to support its claims. Back of it are all the wealth and prestige of the realm. Back of it is the life of every patriotic citizen. Back of it are all the alliances with friendly powers. The throne of grace means that GOD is now ruling in the power of His love, and we have access to that power."[28]

"Come close to God, and God will come close to you" (James 4:8 NLT). The word "come" bespeaks a royal invitation to meet with God in the chamber of prayer. Scriptural invitations to pray are numerous and include "Come unto me, all ye that labor and are heavy laden, and I will give you rest" (Matthew 11:28); "Do not be anxious about anything, but in everything by prayer and supplication with thanksgiving let your requests be made known to God" (Philippians 4:6 ESV); "Seek the Lord and his strength; seek his presence continually" (1 Chronicles 16:11 ESV); "If you abide in me, and my words abide in you, ask whatever you wish, and it will be done for you" (John 15:7 ESV); "The Lord is near to all who call on him, to all who call on him in truth" (Psalm 145:18 ESV); and "Call unto me, and I will answer thee, and shew thee great and mighty things, which thou knowest not" (Jeremiah 33:3).

A. W. Pink says the first phrase of the Lord's prayer "informs us in the simplest possible manner that the great God is most graciously ready to grant us an audience. By directing us to address Him as our Father, it definitely assures us of His love and power. This precious title is designed to raise our affections, to excite us to reverent attention, and to confirm our confidence in the efficacy of prayer."[29]

> There's a garden where Jesus is waiting,
>   And He bids you to come meet Him there,
> Just to bow and receive a new blessing,
>   In the beautiful garden of prayer.
> ~ Eleanor Allen Schroll (1920)

"The value of prayer," wrote E. M. Bounds, "does not lie in the number of prayers or the length of prayers, but its value is found in the great truth that we are privileged by our relations to God to unburden our desires and make our requests known to God, and He will relieve by granting our petitions."[30] The welcome mat at the "throne of grace" is always out for the believer, granting him access to the presence of God with his every care and need. Saith Spurgeon, "The very invitation to us to pray implies that there are blessings waiting for us at the mercy seat: 'Let us therefore come boldly unto the throne of grace.'"[31]

Chapter 4

Why Pray?

"Our prayers lay the track down which God's power can come. Like a mighty locomotive, His power is irresistible, but it cannot reach us without rails."[32] ~ Watchman Nee

Why pray? The preeminent intention of prayer is found in Jesus' prayer in John 12 when He said, "Father, glorify thy name" (John 12:28). R. C. Sproul said, "Prayer, like everything else in the Christian life, is for God's glory and for our benefit, in that order."[33] Ole Hallesby said, "Prayer is ordained for the purpose of glorifying the name of God. Therefore, whether you pray for big things or for little things, say to God, 'If it will glorify Thy name, then grant my prayer and help me. But if it will not glorify Thy name, then let me remain in my predicament and give me power to glorify Thy name in the situation in which I find myself.'"[34] Hallesby continued, "Nothing makes us so bold in prayer as when we can look into the eye of God and say to Him, 'Thou knowest that I am not praying for personal advantage, nor to avoid hardship, nor that my own will in any way should be done, but only for this, that Thy name might be glorified.'"[35]

Why pray? Spurgeon says, "We do not bow the knee merely because it is a duty and a commendable spiritual exercise, but because we believe that into the ear of the eternal God we speak our wants, and that His ear is linked with a heart feeling for us and a hand working on our behalf. To us, true prayer is true power."[36]

Why pray? We pray out of obedience to the Lord (Luke 18:1 and 1 Timothy 2:8). Jesus mandated prayer numerous times: "Ask, and it will be given to you; seek, and you will find; knock, and it will be opened to you" (Matthew 7:7 ESV); "Again I say to you, if two of you agree on earth about anything they ask, it will be done" (Matthew 18:19 ESV); "It is written, 'My house shall be called a house of prayer'" (Matthew 21:13 ESV); "Pray earnestly to the Lord of the harvest to send out laborers" (Luke 10:2 ESV); "Men ought always to pray, and not to faint" (Luke 18:1); "Pray that you may not enter into temptation" (Luke 22:40 ESV); "If you abide in me, and my words abide in you, ask whatever you wish, and it will be done for you" (John 15:7 ESV); "Ask, and you will receive" (John

16:24 ESV); "Pray without ceasing" (1 Thessalonians 5:17); "Enter into thy closet, and when thou hast shut thy door, pray to thy Father" (Matthew 6:6); "Is any among you afflicted? let him pray" (James 5:13). We pray, for it is part of worship to Him (Psalm 95:6–7). We pray to have an intimate connection to and communion with God. We pray, for it is God's appointed means of receiving good things at His hand (Ezekiel 36:37 and Luke 11:13). We pray to obtain grace and mercy for every need (Hebrews 4:16). Through prayer the believer obtains (not simply requests) mercy (cleansing and pardon of sin—a continual need) and the benefits of the riches of God's grace (the supernatural power of God to supply mercy, comfort, consolation, strength, counsel, healing, peace, etc.).

Why pray? Because prayer is an exchange: "We leave our burdens, worries and sin in the hands of God. We come away with the oil of joy and the garment of praise."[37] We pray, for God has attached divine promises to prayer (Matthew 7:7) that can be claimed only through engaging in it.

Why pray? Believers pray to acquire the power of the Holy Spirit to live victoriously over "the lust of the flesh, and the lust of the eyes, and the pride of life" (1 John 2:16) and to defeat the wiles (tactics, strategies) of the Devil (Ephesians 6:11). Saith Spurgeon, "Prayer brings inner strength to God's warriors and sends them forth to spiritual battle with their muscles firm and their armor in place."[38] E. Stanley Jones said, "When prayer fades out, power fades out. We are as spiritual as we are prayerful—no more, no less."[39]

Prayer, the Christian's mightiest weapon against Satan, thwarts his plans, blocks his work, and forces his retreat. Hindering prayer is Satan's mightiest weapon against the Christian. We pray so we may partner with God in the advancement of His kingdom on earth (Matthew 6:10; 9:37–38).

Jonathan Edwards said, "There is no way that Christians, in a private capacity, can do so much to promote the work of

God and advance the kingdom of Christ as by prayer."[40] D. L. Moody said, "Behind every work of God, you will always find a kneeling form."[41] Andrew Murray wrote, "God rules the world and His church through the prayers of His people. That God should have made the extension of His Kingdom to such a large extent dependent on the faithfulness of His people in prayer is a stupendous mystery and yet an absolute certainty."[42] In agreement, E. M. Bounds, says, "God shapes the world by prayer. The more praying there is in the world, the better the world will be, the mightier the forces against evil."[43] D. L. Moody said, "Those who have left the deepest impression on this sin-cursed earth have been men and women of prayer."[44]

We pray to break down the strongholds of Satan, thwart his devious and malicious work, and drive him back from the ground he has gained in the church, Christian work, and lives. Spurgeon said, "Even as the moon influences the tides of the sea, even so does prayer influence the tides of godliness."[45]

Why pray? Pray to thrust needed workers into the harvest (Matthew 9:38). A. B. Simpson says, "Prayer is the mighty engine that is to move the missionary work."[46]

Why pray? We pray to solicit the power and grace of God to bind up the brokenhearted; to set the prisoner free; to comfort all that mourn, by giving them beauty for ashes and the garment of praise for the spirit of heaviness (Isaiah 61:1–3).

Why pray? To nourish and sustain the soul. Saith Andrew Bonar, "In order to grow in grace, we must spend a great deal of time in quiet solitude. Contact with others is not what causes the soul to grow most vigorously. In fact, one quiet hour of prayer will often yield greater results than many days spent in the company of others."[47]

Why pray? Saith Thomas A. Tarrants, "Because the Sovereign God, who is indeed omniscient, omnipotent, and good, has established prayer as the means by which we receive what He has promised and help fulfill what He has ordained."[48]

Why pray? We pray, for it is the means of the most supreme joy and delight. David testified that time spent in communion and fellowship with the Lord filled him with "great" authentic joy. He says, "The LORD is my strength and my shield; my heart trusted in him, and I am helped: therefore my heart greatly rejoiceth; and with my song will I praise him" (Psalm 28:7). Prayer is a joy, brings joy. "Until now you have not asked for anything in my name. Ask and you will receive, and your joy will be complete" (John 16:24 NIV). Tim Keller says, "A triune God would call us to converse with Him...because He wants to share the joy He has. Prayer is our way of entering into the happiness of God Himself."[49] George Müller remarks, "The joy which answers to prayer give cannot be described, and the impetus which they afford to the spiritual life is exceedingly great."[50] Spurgeon stated, "Prevalence with God in wrestling prayer is sure to make the believer strong— if not happy. The nearest place to the gate of Heaven is the throne of the heavenly grace. Much alone, and you will have much assurance; little alone with Jesus, your religion will be shallow, polluted with many doubts and fears, and not sparkling with the joy of the Lord."[51]

Why pray? We pray because prayer changes things. Schauffler says, "When we are on our knees, then light flashes; then the intellect is clarified; then the conscience is aroused; then the spiritual sensibilities are quickened, and we can learn more of our duty and of His will than in hours of argumentation."[52]

Why pray? John Calvin states: "Words fail to explain how necessary prayer is and in how many ways the exercise of prayer is profitable. Surely with good reason the Heavenly Father affirms that the only stronghold of safety is in calling upon his name."[53]

Why pray? John Wesley answers, "It seems that God is limited by our prayer life. He can do nothing for humanity unless someone asks Him."[54]

Chapter 5

Three Elements of Prayer

"The man who truly prays gets from God many things denied the prayerless man."[55] ~ E. M. Bounds

S. D. Gordon says prayers need three things: "First an ear to hear what God says, then a tongue to speak, then an eye to watch for the result."[56] The reading of the Holy Scriptures is the hearing aspect. Andrew Murray states, "God's Word supplies us with material for prayer and encourages us in expecting everything from God."[57] It boosts confidence in praying. John MacArthur said, "I believe prayer works. I believe prayer is effective, because there is a record of its effectiveness revealed in Scripture."[58]

The speaking part is taking that which you have heard and personalizing it unto God in prayer. And the seeing component is connecting that which happens with what was prayed. We read that Elijah prayed for rain and then sent his servant to look to see if there were any cloud formations in the sky. He prayed for rain seven times, and seven times he had his servant look for rain clouds. Finally, on the seventh time, the servant reported, "Behold, there ariseth a little cloud out of the sea, like a man's hand" (1 Kings 18:44). With that news Elijah knew his prayers had been answered. Connect what happens in your life with that for which you prayed. It will impact your faith mightily in the efficacy of prayer.

Chapter 6

Pattern for Prayer

"When you pray the seven petitions of the Lord's Prayer, you've prayed for every area of your life, and you've also prayed in every way expected by God."[59] ~ David Yonggi Cho

The disciple's prayer, known to many as the "Lord's Prayer," of Matthew 6 serves as a pattern on which to base prayer. "After this manner," or "like this" (Matthew 6:9), indicates that what followed was not to be a rigid form of prayer but a guide, a model.[60] William MacDonald says, "It was not given as the exact words they were to use [Matthew 6:7 seems to rule this out], because many words repeated by rote memory can become empty phrases."[61] Leon Morris states that the point of the prayer is to give assistance in fashioning personal prayers.[62] Used in a heartfelt manner, not mechanically, the model prayer can be meaningful and powerful, even uttered verbatim. Abuse of it by some in an empty, Pharisaic repetition should not prevent it from being used in a thoughtful and guarded way as a part of church and family worship.

Saith A. W. Pink, "The soul must solemnly remind itself of Who it is that is to be approached, even the Most High, before whom the very seraphim veil their faces."[63] Prayer is to be directed to God, not to saints or angels or their statues and pictures. We are to address prayer only to the One who is "our Father which art in heaven" (Matthew 6:9). The title indicates an intimate relationship between God and His children that was brought about redemptively through the new birth (John 1:12; Romans 8:15) made possible through the sacrificial death of Christ at Calvary. "There is no direct thought here of God as the All-Father in the modern and often deistic sense."[64]

Spurgeon says, "It is a prayer adapted only to those who are the possessors of grace and are truly converted. In the lips of an ungodly man, it is entirely out of place."[65] Adam Clarke comments, "The word 'Father,' placed here at the beginning of this prayer, includes two grand ideas which should serve as a foundation to all our petitions: that tender and respectful love which we should feel for God, such as that which children feel for their fathers; and that strong confidence in God's love to us, such as fathers have for their children."[66] Saith Matthew Henry, "If he be our Father, He will pity us under our weaknesses and infirmities...will deny us nothing that is good for us"[67]—and grant us bold access to Himself, as to a father.[68]

Let us come to the Throne Room by prayer to Him that is our Father and Friend; the King eternal, immortal, invisible; the only wise God; the maker and sustainer of all that is; who upholds all things by the word of His power; in whom we live, and move, and have our being; and who is rich in mercy and bountiful in love and finds great pleasure in bestowing good gifts upon His own—those in Him whose love is indescribable, whose mercy is immeasurable, whose kindness is incomparable, and whose provision is inexhaustible. Knowledge of the Most Holy infuses trust in Him to answer prayer.

"Thou art to commune," saith Spurgeon, "with one who is not like thy fellow men, who may let thee plead and remain like a block, unmoved by thy pathetic requests; but to a living God, a tender God, sensitive to all the sensations of thy soul. Oh, to come before the living and acting God! Not before a God, lame and impotent; nor before the new God, who is impersonal and dead; but before the true God—God in Christ Jesus! If we did but realize who He is to whom we speak— God, very nigh to us in the person of the Only Begotten, who has taken our nature upon Himself—what praying ours would be! And that is the right sort of praying."[69]

Matthew Henry says, "We believe that the God we pray to is a King and a God—King of kings and God of gods—but that is not enough. The most commanding, encouraging principle of prayer, and the most powerful or prevailing plea in prayer, is to look upon him as *our* King and *our* God, to whom we lie under peculiar obligations and from whom we have peculiar expectations."[70]

The prayer presents distinct petitions on which to frame prayer (Matthew 6:9–13).

Pray for God's person to be revered: "Hallowed be Thy name." The priority of prayer is God. A. W. Pink says, "How

14

clearly then is the fundamental duty in prayer set forth. Self and all its needs must be given a secondary place, and the Lord freely accorded the preeminence in our thoughts and supplications. This petition must take the precedence, for the glory of God's great name is the ultimate end of all things."[71] Although God loves us and wants to supply our needs, resolve our problems, and comfort our hurts, He states that our first petition in prayer is to be about Him, to give honor and praise to Him (Matthew 6:9). We are to "hallow" His name before we make petition for ourselves and others. To hallow His name is to give praise for who He is, His attributes (mercy, grace, love, forgiveness, patience, goodness, etc.) and marvelous works. It is to hold Him in reverence and holy awe.[72] It is to pray that God Himself will cause His name "to be known and adored through the preaching of the Gospel and be sanctified and magnified in and by us."[73] John Calvin said, "That God's name should be hallowed is to say that God should have His own honor of which He is so worthy, so that men should never think or speak of Him without the greatest veneration."[74] To quote Pink again: "All real prayer ought to begin with a devout contemplation and to express an acknowledgment of the name of God and of His blessed perfections. We should draw near unto the Throne of Grace with suitable apprehensions of God's sovereign majesty and power, yet with a holy confidence in His fatherly goodness."[75] Too much sloppy sentimentalism accompanies some prayer. To use terms like "my good buddy" or "the big man upstairs" in reference to God, or even to overplay the term "daddy," is belittling to His holiness and name. Our first and foremost duty in prayer is that "God in all things may be glorified" (1 Peter 4:11).

Pray for God's program to be expanded: "Thy kingdom come." Alan Redpath said, "Before we can pray, 'Thy Kingdom come,' we must be willing to pray, 'My kingdom go.'"[76] Matthew Henry comments, "Let the Gospel be preached to all and embraced by all; let all be brought to subscribe to the record God has given in His Word concerning

His Son, and to embrace Him as their Savior and Sovereign. Let the bounds of the Gospel church be enlarged, the kingdom of the world be made Christ's."[77]

Pray for God's plan to be accomplished: "Thy will be done." The heart of the Lord's prayer is that God's will may become the rule of our conduct and actions. John Stott notes, "What Jesus bids us pray is that life on earth may come to approximate more nearly to life in Heaven."[78]

Pray for God's provision to be supplied: "Give us this day our daily bread." The "daily bread" to Luther was a symbol for "everything necessary for the preservation of this life, like food, a healthy body, good weather, house, home, wife, children, good government, and peace."[79]

Pray for God's pardon to be known: "Forgive us our debts as we forgive our debtors." No believer has prayed his last prayer for divine forgiveness, nor will he until he reaches Heaven. John Stott says, "Sin is likened to a 'debt' because it deserves to be punished. But when God forgives sin, He remits the penalty and drops the charge against us."[80] When we request forgiveness, our Lord takes our sin and puts it in the depth of the sea, to remember it against us no more (Micah 7:19 and 1 John 1:9). "By this prayer we are reminded of our constant liability to sin"[81]—and, I add, God's willingness to forgive it.

Pray for God's protection to be experienced: "And lead us not into temptation, but deliver us from evil." That is, deliver us from "the evil one," Satan, who as a roaring lion seeketh to destroy us through various tactics and besetting temptations (1 Peter 5:8). Matthew Henry states, "Temptations are to be prayed against, both because of the discomfort and trouble of them, and because of the danger we are in of being overcome by them, and the guilt and grief that then follow."[82] In battling temptation, the arm of flesh must not be trusted to thwart it, but utter reliance upon Christ alone (1 John 4:4).

"While praying not to be led into temptation," saith Winslow, "we should be watchful against voluntarily running into it."[83]

> God wills not that His people
> By sin enthralled shall be,
> But that their lives, as ransomed,
> Be lives of victory;
>
> And so at our disposal
> He places all His power,
> That we from its resources
> May draw in danger's hour. ~ W. A. Garratt

Pray for God's praise to be exhibited: "For thine is the Kingdom, and the power, and the glory, forever." Saith Vaughan, "All prayer should gather itself up and crown itself in praise."[84] A. W. Pink reminds us, "Unless we express gratitude for mercies already received and give thanks to our Father for His granting us the continued favor of petitioning Him, how can we expect to obtain His ear and thus to receive answers of peace? Yet prayer, in its highest and fullest sense, rises above thanksgiving for gifts vouchsafed; the heart is drawn out in contemplating the Giver Himself, so that the soul is prostrated before Him in worship and adoration."[85] See Philippians 4:6.

Pray the specific petitions of the prayer one at a time. They are not to be jumbled together or passed over too quickly. Focus upon the "Hallowed be thy name" thoroughly before moving on to "Thy kingdom come." Do this with all the objects of prayer, pray "through" one request thoroughly prior to passing to the next. Spurgeon says in this regard, *"Don't try to put two arrows on the bow at once; they will both miss.* Oh! stop at each request until you have really prayed it. Plead once with God and prevail, and then plead again. Get the first mercy, and then go again for the second."[86] Note: Don't restrict prayer to just health, provision, and well-being issues ("daily bread" requests). Enlarge prayer to include the weightier matters of personal holiness, conformity to the will of God and empowered Christian living (Philippians 1:9–11).

"The Lord's Prayer" (in English) is only about sixty words, and only six sentences. It's not the length of a prayer that counts, but its depth. Spurgeon states, "The best prayers have usually been the shortest. An arrow may easily be too long, and prayers should be like arrows shot from the bow of faith. If they are short, it does not matter, so long as they are sharp and sent on their way with a good pull of the bowstring."[87] Further he said, "God does not hear us because of the length of our prayer, but because of the sincerity of it. Prayer is not to be measured by the yard, nor weighed by the pound. It is the might and force of it, the truth and reality of it, the energy and the intensity of it."[88] John Stott observes, "It is comparatively easy to repeat the words of the Lord's Prayer like a parrot. To pray them with sincerity, however, has revolutionary implications, for it expresses the priorities of a Christian."[89]

Chapter 7

To Pray Only Not to Pray

"Despite all his former superfluity of ostentatious devotion, Saul all his life long had never prayed at all. Until the first brokenhearted confession of sin came from the poor, blinded persecutor of Jesus, the Lord considered that he had never prayed."[90] ~ C. H. Spurgeon

Much praying is not really praying, but is just taken as praying. Although Saul of Taurus (Paul) had prayed all his life as a strict Pharisee, it wasn't until after his conversion that he actually prayed for the first time. "Behold, he prayeth" (Acts 9:11). That Saul's praying was futile and impotent until his conversion, we know for four reasons.

Real prayer is to be based upon access to Heaven's throne through the name of Jesus (Ephesians 2:18). Saul persecuted Christ. He certainly didn't pray in His name.

Real prayer is to be based upon the merit of Christ, not self-righteousness (2 Corinthians 5:21; Romans 5:19). Saul, a strict Pharisee, lived by the Mosaic Law and counted it the means to Heaven's throne through prayer (Philippians 3:5). Our access to God in prayer is to be based upon the imputed righteousness of Christ in man, not his own (Romans 4:22; 2 Corinthians 5:21). Spurgeon said, "It is a great thing to conquer sinful self, but it is a greater thing to overcome righteous self. The man who is downright bad and feels it asks for mercy, but [the self-righteous] are bad at heart and do not feel it; therefore, they will not seek the Lord."[91]

Real prayer is to be based upon humility. Saul prayed haughtily. He, like the Pharisee in the Temple, boasted in prayer of good deeds and superiority to other men (Luke 18:11–14). James says, "God opposes the proud but shows favor to the humble" (James 4:6 NIV). The prayer that God hears is, "God be merciful to me a sinner" (Luke 18:13). It is the prayer of confession and contrition, not self-commendation and praise.

Real prayer is to be based upon a right heart. See Psalm 24:4 and 2 Timothy 2:22. Saul's heart was ungodly and defiled by sin. The Bible says, "The LORD is far from the wicked: but he heareth the prayer of the righteous" (Proverbs 15:29); and, "Now we know that God heareth not sinners" (John 9:31). Spurgeon comments, "If you are living an ungodly life, I do not care how regularly you bend your knee in seeming devotion; there is nothing in it."[92]

Saul's empty praying was changed into true prayer at the moment of his salvation on the Damascus Road. Unless prayer is uttered from a regenerate heart, it has no wings on which to ascend to Heaven and thus is in vain (Ephesians 2:18). Saith Spurgeon, "'Behold, he prayeth' is a surer witness of a man's conversion than, 'Behold, he singeth or readeth the Scripture or preacheth.' These things may be admirably done by men who are not regenerate; but if a man *really* prays, we may know that he has passed from death unto life. Prayer is the autograph of the Holy Ghost upon the renewed heart."[93]

Might it be that like Saul you have religiously "prayed" all of your life—the reciting of prayer beads; lighting of candles; voicing memorized, written, repetitious prayers, and personal utterances without praying? Might it be you are like the Pharisee in the Temple (Luke 18:11–12) who went frequently to the right place to pray ("before God") and thought he did pray, yet did not (evidenced by departing the prayer time without being changed)?

Saith Spurgeon, "The nearer the church, sometimes, the farther from God; and in the very center of it, in the midst of the assembly where prayer is wont to be made, you may not be 'before God' at all. Praying before God is a more spiritual business than is to be performed by turning to the east or to the west, or bowing the knee, or entering within walls hallowed for ages. Alas! It is easy enough to pray and not to pray before God."[94] It's most difficult for a man that has prayed wrongly, blindly, and ignorantly, though sincerely, all his life to begin praying rightly. But it is possible. Just ask Saul.

The sinner's first prayer, "Lord, be merciful to be a sinner and save me for Thy name's sake," grants him continuous access to God (Hebrews 4:16).

To the surprise of some, Christians might also pray without praying (Jeremiah 11:11; Lamentations 3:42–44). Prayers are mere words in the wind when cold, formal, heartless, and voiced for the admiration of men or from an unclean heart ("If I regard iniquity in my heart, the Lord will not hear me" [Psalm 66:18]).

You may often pray, BUT do you pray when you pray?

Chapter 8

Simplicity of Prayer

"The main lesson of prayer is just this: Do it! Do it! Do it! You want to be taught to pray. My answer is pray and never faint, and then you shall never fail. A sense of real want is the very root of prayer."[95] ~ John Laidlaw

Prayer is so simple that even a child can pray, be heard, and receive an answer. Don't make complicated that which God made simple. Saith Spurgeon, "No doubt by praying we learn to pray; and the more we pray, the oftener we can pray, and the better we can pray."[96] See Colossians 4:2. The equipment for prayer is simple. "It consists particularly of a quiet place, a quiet hour and a quiet heart"[97]—and a quest to meet with God which is initiated by calling unto Him ("Call unto me" [Jeremiah 33:3]). Ole Hallesby states, "To pray is nothing more involved than to let Jesus into our needs. To pray is to give Jesus permission to employ His powers in the alleviation of our distress. To pray is to let Jesus glorify His name in the midst of our needs."[98]

Samuel Chadwick says, "Fathers and children do not make speeches to each other. God is not far off. He is near. He does not need to be informed, for Jesus says, 'For your Father knoweth what things ye have need of, before ye ask him.' Neither does He need to be persuaded; for 'if ye then, being evil, know how to give good gifts unto your children, how much more shall your Father which is in heaven give good things to them that ask him?' Nothing could be simpler, more natural, more assuring. 'Ask, and ye shall receive, for every one that asketh receiveth.'"[99]

Prayer is the simplest form of speech
    That infant lips can try,
Prayer the sublimest strains that reach
    The Majesty on high. ~ James Montgomery (1818)

With all the books and sermons on prayer, it's easy to adapt methodology that may work for others but is burdensome and ineffective for you. You don't have to jump through a series of hoops or follow a manual step by step each time you pray. Just pray. Remember, as A. W. Tozer said, "The key to prayer is simply praying."[100] Saith Brother Lawrence, "Act with God in the greatest simplicity; speak to Him frankly and plainly."[101] The word "confidence" in 1 John 5:14 means "freedom or frankness in speaking, the freedom to speak one's mind."[102] Simply tell God everything; ask Him for anything that is according to His will. He invites candidness (Hebrews 4:16).

> Steps and guides for praying,
>   Helpful they may be;
> Guard against entanglement
>   In their ABCs.
>
> At times it's best to ban the "plan"
>   And just get on the knees,
> To come to Jesus simply
>   With one's most earnest pleas. ~ Frank Shivers (2022)

If your rule or standard of praying isn't working, is void of life and passion after months of endeavor, it's in need of modification.

Chapter 9

Get Ready to Pray

"Each time you intercede, be quiet first and worship God in His glory. Think of what He can do, of how He delights to hear Christ, of your place in Christ, and expect great things."[103] ~ Andrew Murray

While instructed to pray, we are not to do so hurriedly and unpreparedly. Preparation to pray (not to be a complicated or lengthy process) centers upon several requisites.

First, it hinges upon reverence and humility (Psalm 95:6; Hebrews 12:28; Isaiah 45:23). B. C. Caffin said, "There can be no true prayer without reverence, without a deep sense of God's awful holiness and our utter unworthiness."[104] Remember, therefore, into whose presence thou art entering in prayer— "The high and lofty One" (Isaiah 57:15)—and enter not flippantly, thoughtlessly or rashly, but reverently. "Put off thy shoes from off thy feet" (Exodus 3:5). Daniel (Daniel 6:10); Solomon (2 Chronicles 6:13); Peter (Acts 9:40); Paul (Acts 21:5; Acts 20:36; Ephesians 3:14); and Stephen (Acts 7:60) exhibited grave reverence in prayer.

Second, it hinges upon confession of and cleansing from sin (Psalm 24:3–5; 1 John 1:9; Psalm 139:23–24). Spurgeon writes, "Nothing hinders prayer like iniquity harbored in the heart; as with Cain, so with us, sin lies at the door and blocks the passage. If you refuse to hear God's commands, He will surely refuse to hear your prayers."[105] See Psalm 66:18. J. I. Packer said, "The efficacy of prayer depends on uprightness of life and motive, wholehearted and sustained earnestness in the person praying, and how far it conforms to God's revealed purposes and ways."[106]

In the third place, it is contingent upon setting the heart in tune with a readiness to pray. Robert Murray McCheyne said, "Study your prayers; a great part of my time is spent getting in tune for prayer."[107] Adam Clarke says, "Prayer requires more of the heart than of the tongue."[108] Approach God in quietude. Saith Ole Hallesby, "This attitude can be compared to a forerunner who announces the coming of God to us. In this too we see God's gracious dealings. It is His divine presence which attunes our distracted, worldly, and earthly-minded souls to prayer. Many who pray are not aware of this. As soon as they enter into their secret chamber they begin at once to speak with God. Do not do that, my friend. Take plenty of time before you begin to speak. Let quietude wield its influence upon you. Let the fact that you are alone assert itself. Give your soul time to get released from the many outward things. Give God time to play the prelude to prayer for the benefit of your distracted soul."[109]

To ready the heart for prayer, R. A. Torrey writes, "The first thing that we should do is to see to it that we really get an audience with God, that we really get into His very presence. Before a word of petition is offered, we should have the definite and vivid consciousness that we are talking to God and should believe that He is listening to our petition and is going to grant the thing that we ask of Him."[110]

And prayer preparation involves forethought about the who, what and why of the praying. Too often we chase "rabbits" or ramble in prayer, failing to make explicit requests. It's haphazardly engaged in. Ponder all to be requested prior to kneeling (other matters may surface in prayer). In prayer don't be like the man that goes to the store without a shopping list, only to leave without the most needful items.

And to ready the heart for prayer, come clothed in boldness and faith. Saith A. W. Tozer: "When entering the prayer chamber, we must come filled with faith and armed with courage. Nowhere else in the whole field of religious thought and activity is courage so necessary as in prayer. The successful prayer must be one without condition. We must believe that God is love and that, being love, He cannot harm us but must ever do us good. Then we must throw ourselves before Him and pray with boldness for whatever we know our good and His glory require, and the cost is no object! Whatever He in His love and wisdom would assess against us, we will accept with delight because it pleased Him. Prayers like that cannot go unanswered. The character and reputation of God guarantee their fulfillment. No one need fear to put his life in His hands."[111]

Live in much readiness to pray at any moment by walking in devotedness and holiness to Christ (John 15:4–7), in the Spirit (Galatians 5:16), in obedience to Christ (1 John 3:21–22), in reverence to Christ (Revelation 4:10), in an attitude of prayer (1 Thessalonians 5:17), and in purity of heart (1 John 1:9).

Chapter 10
In the Name of Jesus

"To pray in Jesus' name means to acknowledge that we only have access to the Father's attention and grace through the mediation and work of our Savior."[112] ~ Tim Keller

Paul states, "For through him [Christ Jesus] we both have access by one Spirit unto the Father" (Ephesians 2:18). Authority, or the right, to be called the sons of God and gain access to His throne through prayer is granted to all who confess Jesus as Lord and Savior through repentance and faith. How is this possible? At the moment of salvation, a person receives the imputed righteousness of Christ, the righteousness or perfection of Jesus, and it is this that grants him full access to "the throne of grace" with confidence that requests will be heard and answered (Hebrews 4:16).

To elucidate, when we appear before the throne of God, it's not the believer's wretchedness that is seen, but rather the uprightness of Jesus; and it is that which grants the access. This "imputation" was made possible through Jesus' death (atoning work) at Calvary, and subsequent resurrection.

To pray in Jesus' name is to pray as Jesus might pray, consistent with His desire, will, and the Scripture (to ask as if He were asking). To pray in Jesus' name is to pray on the basis of the authorization He has given us to make our petitions known to the Father (as in John 14:14: "If ye shall ask anything in *My name*, I will do it.") Saith Spurgeon: "If you send a child or servant to a friend for a thing in your name, the request is yours; and he that denieth the child or servant denieth you. Jesus Christ hath bidden you ask in His name, so that in effect your request becomes Christ's request. God can no more deny your request in Christ's name than he can deny Christ himself. This is the true meaning of asking in Christ's name. It is a higher plea than 'for Jesus' sake.'"[113]

Saith Warren Wiersbe, "Great names come and go, but the name of Jesus remains. The Devil still hates it, the world still opposes it, but God still blesses it; and we can still claim it! 'In the name of Jesus' is the key that unlocks the door of prayer and the treasury of God's grace. It's the weapon that defeats the enemy, and the motivation that compels our sacrifice and service. It's the name that causes our hearts to rejoice and our lips to sing his praise."[114]

As the Gaither's say, "Jesus, Jesus, Jesus—there's just something about that name!" Let's use it properly, reverently, meaningfully, and authoritatively. Don't invoke Jesus' name in prayer as a magical charm. Don't simply tack the phrase to the end of a prayer.

> Thy name, O Jesus, beckons me;
> That trusting I shall come to Thee,
> In faith and love on Thee lay hold
> And deep within my heart enfold.
>
> I call upon Thy name each day,
> Where'er on earth I wander may;
> It is for me a house of peace
> Where from all grief I find release.[115]
>
> ~ Translation by P. A. Sveeggen

Though spoken over a century ago, the advice given by Bishop Hall regarding prayer is extremely timely: "Remember, the Lord will not hear you because of the arithmetic of your prayers, counting their numbers. He will not hear you because of the rhetoric of your prayers, caring for the eloquent language in which they are conveyed. He will not listen because of the geometry of your prayers, computing them by their length or breadth. He will not regard you because of the music of your prayers, caring for sweet voices or for harmony. Neither will He look at you because of the logic of your prayers, because they are well arranged and excellently divided. But He will hear you, and He will measure the number of blessings He will give you, according to the divinity of your prayers. If you can plead the person of Christ, and if the Holy Ghost inspires you with zeal and earnestness, the blessings that you shall ask shall surely come to you."[116]

The Bottom Line: Christians close their prayer by saying "in Jesus' name" because man's sinful nature prohibits access to a holy God through any other means: "For there is one God, and one mediator [bridge] between God and men, the man Christ Jesus" (1 Timothy 2:5). It is the means of receiving that for which we ask (John 14:13) and is praying (asking) in agreement with the desire and will of Jesus. Hallesby wrote, "Nothing means so much to our daily prayer life as to pray in the name of Jesus. If we fail to do this, our prayer life will either die from discouragement and despair or become simply a duty which we feel we must perform."[117]

Join Spurgeon in praying: "Lord Jesus, cause me to know in my daily experience the glory and sweetness of Thy name, and then teach me how to use it in my prayer, so that I may be even like Jacob, a prince prevailing with God. Thy name is my passport and secures me access; Thy name is my plea and secures me answer; Thy name is my honor and secures me glory."[118] In Jesus' name, Amen.

Chapter 11

The Holy Spirit's Role

"Prayer is the key to Heaven; the Spirit helps faith turn this key."[119] ~ Thomas Watson

The Holy Spirit, through the finished work of Christ at Calvary, grants the Christian access to God through prayer (Ephesians 2:18), sanctifies prayer, influences what to say in prayer, prompts prayer, convinces of the efficacy of prayer, assists in prayer, reminds us of promises to plead in prayer and arguments to make before God based on them, grants importunity in prayer, and secures success in prayer. Spurgeon, speaking of the Spirit's intercession for the saint, says, "We fall into such heaviness of spirit and entanglement of thought that the one remedy of prayer, which we have always found to be unfailing, appears to be taken from us. Here, then, in the nick of time, as a very present help in time of trouble, comes in the Holy Spirit. He draws near to teach us how to pray, and in this way, He helps our infirmity, relieves our suffering, and enables us to bear the heavy burden without fainting under the load."[120] See Romans 8:26. It is the Spirit that prompts the subject of our praying.

Prayer is impossible without the Spirit's help from beginning to end (Jude 20). This is why believers are instructed to 'pray in the Holy Spirit,' under His direction and enablement (Ephesians 6:18). "All that is right in our prayers is from the Spirit, and all that is wrong in them from ourselves."[121] D. Moore says, "Praying in the Spirit, therefore, is to pray in that spirit of grace and supplication which the Holy Ghost alone can bestow—to pray in that 'spirit of adoption, whereby we cry, Abba, Father!' And further, by praying in the Spirit is meant that we should pray in a right mind, that we should pray fervently, that we should pray with a consciousness that there is an assisting Power to help us."[122] Adrian Rogers tells us, "Praying in the Spirit will change prayer from a weary grudge to a delightsome privilege."[123]

The Mighty Acts of the Holy Spirit and Prayer

The work of the Holy Spirit in the Book of Acts was associated with prayer. When His power was sought, He wrought great works. When it wasn't, naught was accomplished. The saints prayed in preparation for the coming of the Holy Spirit (Acts 1:14), and afterward three thousand souls were saved through a single sermon (Acts 2:41), and the New Testament church was born. When the members of that new body devoted themselves to prayer (Acts 2:42), the church grew rapidly. Soon the threat of persecution for their belief and practice arose, driving them to their knees. As they prayed, they "were all filled with the Holy Spirit and spoke the word of God boldly" (Acts 4:31 NIV). Later, when Peter was arrested, placed into prison and sentenced to die, the church prayed on his behalf; and God sent an angel to deliver him (Acts 12:5–11). It was through prayer that the Holy Spirit sent out Paul and Barnabas into the Roman world as missionaries (Acts 13:1–3) and did mighty works through them (Acts 16:16–18; Acts 19:11). At every turning point in the development of the New Testament church, the saints tapped the power of the Holy Spirit to grant them success in their endeavors.

> Come, Holy Spirit; dark is the hour.
> We need Your filling, Your love and Your mighty power.
> Move now among us; stir us we pray.
> Come, Holy Spirit; revive the church today.
> ~ John W. Peterson

The wheels of the church and kingdom ministry turn upon the work of the Holy Spirit in response to prayer. They always have. They always will. John Stott said, "What we need is not more learning, not more eloquence, not more persuasion, not more organization, but more power from the Holy Spirit." Amen. Pray for the power of the Holy Spirit to be unleashed in the church, the world and your life (Luke 11:13).

Chapter 12

Common Errors in Prayer

"The believer should not make a show of his prayer, nor of the answers he receives to prayer, in such a way as to call unnecessary attention to himself."[124] ~ Hindson and Kroll

In Matthew 6:5–15, Jesus points out three common errors concerning prayer.

The first is praying to be heard by others (Matthew 6:5–6). Prayer is not to be a display of self-righteousness to gain the admiration of others.[125] It is not to be shaped for public viewing. Guard against the ostentatiousness of the Pharisees in prayer, that Jesus condemned (Matthew 6:6). Spurgeon said, "Beware of having an eye to the auditors; beware of becoming rhetorical to please the listeners. Remember the people in your prayers, but do not mold your supplications to win their esteem."[126] Proper motivation makes or breaks prayer.

The second error is using "vain repetitions" in prayer (Matthew 6:7). Solomon said, "Be not rash with thy mouth, and let not thine heart be hasty to utter anything before God: for God is in heaven, and thou upon earth: therefore let thy words be few" (Ecclesiastes 5:2). "The warning is against hasty and thoughtless words in prayer, words that go from the lips with glib facility absent of sincerity. Thus, our Lord bids those who pray not to use vain repetitions, as the heathen, who think to be heard for their much speaking."[127] Matthew Henry states, "What we utter before God must come from the heart, and therefore we must not be rash with our mouth. We must...not talk carelessly, as we do to one another, not repeat things over and over, as we do to one another."[128] Any form of heartless praying (memorized, read, repetitious, consisting of empty phrases) is to be avoided, for such are ruinous to prayer. Form prayers are meant to be the springboard to heart generated prayer. Refrain from the use of another man's words (prayers). Samuel Chadwick says, "It is not other people's prayers that make the man of prayer. All true prayer, the prayer that prevails, is personal, intimate, and original."[129] The prayers of Spurgeon, Swindoll, Truett and other giants of the faith may be profitable for personal edification but, they would each attest, are not intended to replace personal supplication to the King.

The third error is praying with unconfessed sin in the heart (Matthew 6:14–15). An unforgiving spirit hinders prayer, as does other sin that is unconfessed and unforsaken. Saith Alexander Whyte, "Every kind of prayer—not intercessory prayer only, which is the highest kind of prayer, but all prayer, from the lowest kind to the highest—is impossible in a life of known and allowed sin."[130] For prayer to be effective, it must be offered correctly. The heart must be free from sinful contamination, and requests are to be asked in faith in Jesus' name based upon God's will out of a heart of sincerity.

Chapter 13

The Master's Standard

"To pray in all places where quietness inviteth—in any house, highway, or street—and to know no street in this city that may not witness that I have not forgotten God and my Savior in it, and that no parish [church] or town where I have been may not say the like."[131] ~ Thomas Browne

Our Lord practiced prayer always and everywhere. The Bible says, "During his days on earth, Christ offered prayers and requests with loud cries and tears as his sacrifices to the one who was able to save him from death. He was heard because of his godly devotion" (Hebrews 5:7 CEB). Jesus prayed alone and in public. He prayed before His baptism and entrance upon public ministry. He prayed in the wilderness. He prayed prior to selecting the twelve disciples. He prayed at Lazarus' grave. He prayed at the Last Supper. He prayed before walking on the water. He prayed prior to teaching the disciples how to pray (the model prayer). He prayed in the Garden of Gethsemane. He prayed upon the Cross. He prayed for Peter. He prayed upon the mountains, like the Mount of Transfiguration. He prayed in a desert place. He prayed before making decisions. He prayed before meals. He prayed before performing healings, and afterwards.

The words "pray" and "prayer" are used at least twenty-five times in the New Testament in reference to Christ (numerous other passages where the words don't occur nevertheless indicate that He prayed).[132]

> He sought the mountain and the loneliest height,
>> For He would meet his Father all alone;
>> And there, with many a tear and many a groan,
> He strove in prayer throughout the long, long night.
>
> Why need He pray, who held by filial right
>> O'er all the world alike of thought and sense
>> The fulness of his Sire's omnipotence?
> Why crave in prayer what was His own by might?
>
> Vain is the question—Christ was man in need;
>> And being man, His duty was to pray.
> The son of God confessed the human need
>> And doubtless asked a blessing every day,
> Nor ceases yet for sinful man to plead,
>> Nor will, till Heaven and earth shall pass away.
>
> ~ Hartley Coleridge (1796–1849)

Christ, as with many other things, has left us in His prayer life, praying always and in every place, an example to imitate. Let us "follow in his steps" (1 Peter 2:21 NIV).

Chapter 14

Jabez: An Example in Prayer

"Spiritual blessings are the best blessings, and those are blessed indeed who are blessed with them."[133]

~ Matthew Henry.

"And Jabez called on the God of Israel, saying, Oh that thou wouldest bless me indeed, and enlarge my coast, and that thine hand might be with me, and that thou wouldest keep me from evil, that it may not grieve me! And God granted him that which he requested" (1 Chronicles 4:10).

Pray like Jabez. Address it to God, expressing humility, faith, fervency, importunity, directness, and thoroughness. But also, *pray as Jabez* (personalize it) with four specific requests.

"Oh that thou wouldest bless me indeed." Implore God to enrich your life to its very best end. Note that Jabez leaves the specific type of blessing requested open-ended. There are things that appear to be blessings that are in fact curses (riches, houses and lands, health, promotions, fame), and things that appear to be curses that in truth are blessings (ill-health, frailty, trial, loss, poverty). Like Jabez, rely upon God to determine the form and measure of blessing to bestow. Saith Spurgeon, "Blessings indeed are such blessings as come from the pierced hand; blessings that come from Calvary's bloody tree, streaming from the Savior's wounded side—thy pardon, thine acceptance, thy spiritual life, thy oneness to Christ, and all that comes of it—these are blessings indeed! Any blessing that comes as the result of the Spirit's work in thy soul is a blessing indeed; though it humbles thee, though it strips thee, though it

kills thee, it is a blessing indeed. Though the harrow goes over and over thy soul and the deep plow cut into thy very heart, though thou be maimed and wounded and left for dead, yet if the Spirit of God do it, it is a blessing indeed."[134] Therefore, advises Spurgeon, "Let the grace of God prompt it, let the choice of God appoint it, let the bounty of God confer it, and then the endowment shall be something godlike indeed."[135]

"Enlarge my coast." None have taken possession of all the territory ordained of God for them to acquire. All live in a self-imposed narrow orbit of devotion, discipline and/or duty, to some degree. Implore God, therefore, with the cry: Enlarge my temporal and spiritual coast. Enlarge my usefulness for the kingdom of God. Enlarge my influence for righteousness. Enlarge my opportunities for service. Enlarge my knowledge of Scripture. Enlarge my profitability to the church and saints. Enlarge my passion for the unsaved. Enlarge my ability to financially aid Thy cause. Enlarge my liberty over the pull of the flesh. Enlarge my heart for prayer and devotional meditation. Enlarge the light of my understanding of Thy will. Enlarge the coast of my ministry. And, most of all, enlarge my heart in greater love for Thee, O Lord (Psalm 119:32).

"That thine hand might be with me." The "mighty hand of God" rescues us, restores us, rebuilds us, reinforces us, restrains us, renews us, and rebuffs us. It is a hand ready to provide grace to sustain in storms, difficulties, sorrow, temptation, adversity, and affliction (Psalm 37:23–24; Isaiah 41:10). It is a hand that guides the direction to go at the crossroads of life (Psalm 123:2). It is a hand that enables His work in us, for us, and through us. It is a hand that gives us our daily bread. As Matthew Henry says, it "is indeed a hand sufficient for us, all-sufficient."[136] With it clutched in our hand, life is a meaningful and happy journey; apart from it all is bleak, hopeless, and futile. This the saint knows from experience and says to God, "I can't even walk without hold-

ing Your hand." Therefore, implore God's hand to be with you always and in all ways.

> Hold to His hand, God's unchanging hand.
> Hold to His hand, God's unchanging hand.
> Build your hopes on things eternal.
> Hold to God's unchanging hand. ~ Jennie Wilson (1906)

"*That thou wouldest keep me from evil.*" Implore God to keep you from sin (the wiles of the Devil and injurious snares of the world) and the painful spoilage and ruin it brings about (Matthew 6:13). Ask of Him enabling empowerment, as Robert Murray McCheyne prayed, to be made "as holy as a pardoned sinner can be."[137]

The answer to Jabez' prayer: "*And God granted him that which he requested.*" Despite the prayer's magnitude, it was immediately and completely granted. Success was given to Jabez, he was shielded from evil, blessings supernal were bestowed upon him, and God's hand of strength rested with him. The God of Jabez is unchanged (Hebrews 13:8). He ever hears and answers prayer. Jabez' prayer is no magic formula to blessing; but when personalized and uttered in the right spirit, it will avail mightily with God.

PART TWO
Principles of Prayer

Chapter 15

The First Rule of Prayer

"The first rule of prayer is not 'faith,' but whether the request is according to God's will."[138] ~ Jim Cymbala

In prayer always add the proviso, "not my will, but thine, be done" (Luke 22:42). James H. Brooks cautions, "Without submission to the will of God as infinitely right and infinitely wise, prayer is not prayer."[139] David Jeremiah says, "Prayer is not to get God to change His will. If we really believe that the will of God is perfect, then why would we want to change it? Our prayers ought to be prompted out of our deep understanding of what the will of God is."[140]

Robert Law has said, "Prayer is a mighty instrument, not for getting man's will done in Heaven, but for getting God's will done in earth."[141] John Stott stated, "Every true prayer is a variation on the theme, 'Your will be done.'"[142] Jon Courson remarked, "The key to prayer is not so much 'name it and claim it.' Rather, the key to prayer is 'request and rest.' That's the way Jesus prayed: 'Father, if it be possible let this cup pass from Me. That's My request. Nevertheless, not My will, but Thy will be done. That's where I will rest.'"[143]

Since answers to prayer are contingent upon praying in the will of God (1 John 5:14–15), it's expedient to know the several ways in which it might be known.

Holy Scripture makes known God's will. God's will always doth align with His Word. Base prayer upon sound doctrine (a text taken out of context is a pretext).

Circumstances of life make known God's will. Open and closed doors, health, abilities, giftedness, and past success in certain undertakings may serve as signs to understanding the mind and will of God. For example, it's extremely unlikely that it's God's will for a 90-year-old invalid to serve as a traveling missionary in Iraq, or for a person who cannot sing to be called to a position in a music ministry. However, circumstances mustn't be relied upon alone; verify that which they seem to indicate with the confirmation of the Holy Spirit and, if possible, the Word of God.

The Holy Spirit makes known God's will. A major role of the Holy Spirit is to guide us in the knowledge of God's will (John 16:13). He is omniscient, omnipresent, and infallible, and therefore most qualified. He never has disappointed or led astray the believer who has sought His counsel wholeheartedly through prayer; therefore, He is to be trusted. Scripture testifies to the work of the Spirit in making known the will of God. Paul and Silas were stopped from going to Bithynia by the Holy Spirit (Acts 16:7), Philip was prompted by the Spirit to witness to the Ethiopian in the chariot (Acts 8:29), and Paul and Barnabas were called to missionary service by the Spirit (Acts 13:2).

It's irrefutable that the Holy Spirit "yet speaketh" to him that hath ears to hear the mind of God. Sometimes He reveals God's will regarding a certain action through impressions to the mind (inner voice of the Spirit) which clearly, unmistakably say, "This is the way, walk ye in it." Sometimes He indicates it through the illumination of a particular scriptural text. Sometimes He manifests it through ministers, family, or friends. Sometimes the Holy Spirit makes it known through a sermon or a book. And sometimes He reveals it through open and shut doors, as noted previously. In each of these ways the Spirit makes known to the believer the will of God, that about which he may pray confidently. Apart from the Spirit's illumination and prompting, we would often be left to pray in ignorance of God's will and to walk in darkness concerning it.

Spiritual markers make known God's will. After living in Egypt, Abraham returned to the place where he had previously called upon the name of the Lord (Genesis 13:3–4). It was a spiritual marker in his life. Spiritual markers are places, reference points which identify a transition, decision, or direction when God clearly gave guidance.[144] In looking at these markers, one can readily see the direction God is moving his life. If that for which you pray seems to mesh with the markers, then it is likely you are praying in the will of God.

The revelation of God's Word, the lenses of one's circumstances, the prompting and confirmation of the Holy Spirit, and the spiritual markers of life enable us to know the will of God about that for which we pray, so that we might pray confidently and expectantly. In matters where the will of God is not clearly discerned, bring it to Him with the proviso, "Thy will be done."

Chapter 16

Flowery Words Not Necessary

"If you can't pray as you want to, pray as you can. God knows what you mean."[145] ~ Vance Havner

Adrian Rogers stated, "We don't pray to impress God. We're not heard for our 'much speaking.' You don't have to use poetic language or be an amateur Shakespeare. If an earthly child can speak to an earthly father, you can speak to your Heavenly Father. We're told to cry out to Him as our Abba—literally translated "Daddy"—Father (Romans 8:15; Galatians 4:6). We're not praying to impress Him."[146] Saith Spurgeon, "We often pray best when we stammer and stutter, and we pray worst when words come rolling like a torrent, one after another. God is not moved by words; they are but a noise to Him. He is only moved by the deep thought and the heaving emotion which dwell in the innermost spirit. What cares He for the grammar?"[147]

A child's words may not be understood by friends, but always are by his mother.[148] Just so, the child of God's prayer, though incomprehensible to another, always is understood by his Heavenly Father. Words used in prayer, though simple and down to earth, don't indicate flippancy, frivolity, or nonchalance. Whatever the vocabulary, exhibit reverence, awe, and honor in God's holy presence. If you feel your prayers are weak and feeble, you're in good company. Spurgeon, the great London pastor, said, "I usually feel more dissatisfied with my prayers than with anything else I do."[149]

Chapter 17

Posture in Prayer

"It pleases God that we bow, that we pray, that we ask, that we talk to Him as our Father. We go further on our knees than in any other way, retreating to advance, falling to rise, stooping to conquer. Oh, the fellowship we have with God in intercession!"[150] ~ W. A. Criswell

To pray upon the knees is favorite posture for many. But if the knees bend apart from the heart bowing, it is unacceptable unto the Lord. Paul liked to pray on his knees (Ephesians 3:14; Acts 20:36), as did Daniel (Daniel 6:10), David (Psalm 95:6), and our beloved Lord and Savior (Luke 22:41). David Livingstone, who also liked to pray kneeling, was found on his knees by his bed at his death. What a way to die!

Scripture indicates other acceptable postures of prayer, including bowing and falling prostrate (Genesis 24:26; Matthew 26:39; Mark 14:35), spreading out the hands (Psalm 28:2; 1 Kings 8:22; 1 Timothy 2:8), and standing

(Mark 11:25; Luke 18:11; 1 Samuel 1:26). In prayer, it's heart posture (Exodus 3:5), not body posture, that is all-important.

"The proper way for a man to pray,"
Said Deacon Lemuel Keyes,
"And the only proper attitude
Is down upon his knees."

"No, I should say the way to pray,"
Said Rev. Doctor Wise,
"Is standing straight with outstretched arms
And rapt and upturned eyes."

"Oh, no; no, no," said Elder Slow,
"Such posture is too proud;
A man should pray with eyes fast closed
And head contritely bowed."

"It seems to me his hands should be
Austerely clasped in front,
With both thumbs pointing toward the ground,"
Said Rev. Doctor Blunt.

"Las' year I fell in Hodgkin's well
Head first," said Cyrus Brown,
"With both my heels a-stickin' up,
My head a-pinting down;

"An' I made a prayer right then an' there—
Best prayer I ever said,
The prayingest prayer I ever prayed,
A-standing on my head." ~ Sam Walter Foss

The right way to pray, simply, saith Dietrich Bonhoeffer, "is to stretch out our hands and ask of One who we know has the heart of a Father."[151]

Chapter 18

Don't Do All the Talking

"If you do all the talking when you pray, how will you ever hear God's answers?"[152] ~ A. W. Tozer

William Barclay said, "The first object of prayer is not so much to speak to God as to listen to Him."[153] Saith Augustine, "Remove from prayer much speaking, not much praying."[154] We enter God's presence and shower Him with praises and petitions. We talk and talk and talk without pausing to let God talk to us, to reveal to us what's on His mind and heart. He wants to speak to us about our ministry. He wants to speak to us about our spiritual walk. He wants to speak to us about sin. He walks to speak to us about His plans for us, to give direction regarding them. He wants to answer our questions. But we don't give Him the chance for our much talking.

"Prayer is not monologue, but dialogue," writes Andrew Murray; "God's voice is its most essential part. Listening to God's voice is the secret of the assurance that He will listen to mine."[155]

T. S. Eliot said, "If we really want to pray, we must first learn to listen, for in the silence of the heart God speaks."[156] Cultivate the habit of listening in prayer. It allows God to draw nigh to you—and you to experience rich fellowship with Him.

> Master, speak! Thy servant heareth,
>   Waiting for Thy gracious word,
> Longing for Thy voice that cheereth;
>   Master, let it now be heard.
> I am list'ning, Lord, for Thee;
> What hast Thou to say to me?

Master, speak! though least and lowest,
    Let me not unheard depart.
Master, speak! For, oh, Thou knowest
    All the yearning of my heart,
Knowest all its truest need;
Speak! and make me blest indeed.

Master, speak! and make me ready,
    When Thy voice is truly heard,
With obedience glad and steady,
    Still to follow every word.
I am listening, Lord, for Thee;
Master, speak, oh, speak to me!

~ Frances Ridley Havergal (1867)

Chapter 19

To Pray Aloud or Silently

"There is music without words; and there is prayer without words. The soul of prayer is being before God and desiring before God, who hears without sounds and understands without expressions. Open your heart, look to Him, and ask Him to read what you cannot read."[157]

~ C. H. Spurgeon

Allan Harmon states, "There is both inaudible prayer to God as well as direct and loud appeals."[158] See Psalm 5:1. Lightfoot says, "It's not of the moving of the lips, but of the elevation of the heart to God that the essence of prayer consists."[159] A prominent televangelist states emphatically that silent or mental prayer is unheard. He is wrong. Although Jesus instructs us to "say" our prayers in the model prayer (Luke 11:2), prayer in solitude may be said mentally.[160] Thomas Aquinas says prayer may be described as "the language of the heart."[161] Prayer is heart communication with

43

God that may be transacted silently or verbally. Spurgeon states, "The voice is not an essential element in prayer. It would be unseemly and impossible to pray aloud unceasingly. The voice is helpful, but not necessary, to the reality or prevalence of prayer."[162] Further, he says, "A silent prayer may have a louder voice than the cries of those priests who sought to awaken Baal with their shouts."[163] Saith Hallesby, "In the soul's fellowship with God in prayer, too, there are things which can and should be formulated in words. But there are also things for which we can find no words. Likely, it is this to which the apostle makes reference when he speaks in Romans 8:26 of the 'groanings which cannot be uttered.'"[164]

Concerning praying with tears, Spurgeon says, "Is it not sweet to believe that our tears are understood even when words fail! Let us learn to think of tears as liquid prayers and of weeping as a constant dropping of importunate intercession which will wear its way right surely into the very heart of mercy, despite the stony difficulties which obstruct the way. My God, I will weep when I cannot plead, for thou hearest the voice of my weeping."[165] See Psalm 6:6–7. Knowing God hears prayers uttered in silence encourages the believer to pray in sundry places in which vocal prayer is not feasible or is prohibited.

Chapter 20

Lifting Up Holy Hands

"The outward symbol of an uplifted heart."[166]

~ A. F. Kirkpatrick

"I lift up my hands toward thy holy oracle" (Psalm 28:2*).* Allan Harman states, "He [the psalmist] has his hands lifted up, as it were, out of the pit, waiting for God to rescue him. Alternatively, here and elsewhere the expression 'to lift up the hands' could be to a posture symbolizing being ready to receive from God an answer to prayer. The 'Most Holy Place' appears to designate the inner sanctuary of the tabernacle/temple, the place that symbolized God's earthly presence."[167] David practiced (Psalms 28:2; 141:2) and advocated the lifting up of hands in prayer (Psalm 134:2). The apostle Paul advocated it: "I will therefore that men pray everywhere, *lifting up holy hands*, without wrath and doubting" (1 Timothy 2:8). Solomon "stood before the altar of the LORD in the presence of all the congregation of Israel, and spread forth his hands toward heaven" (1 Kings 8:22). Following Ezra's reading of God's Law, the entire congregation "answered, Amen, Amen, with lifting up their hands: and they bowed their heads, and worshipped the LORD with their faces to the ground" (Nehemiah 8:6). Ellicott states that the practice seems to have been generally adopted by the early Christians.[168]

The uplifted hand in prayer is symbolic of an uplifted heart and holy disposition that are essential for effectual prayer. The open palms unto the Lord signify that the heart is not embracing or clutching any unclean or unholy thing. Spurgeon remarks that "uplifted hands have always been a form of devout posture and are intended to signify a reaching upward towards God, a readiness, an eagerness to receive the blessing sought after. We stretch out empty hands, for we are beggars; we lift them up, for we seek heavenly supplies; we lift them towards the mercy seat of Jesus, for there our expectation dwells. Oh, that whenever we use devout gestures, we may possess contrite hearts and so speed well with God."[169]

Alexander Maclaren remarks about the lifting up of "holy hands," "One of the Psalms says, 'I will wash mine hands in innocency: so will I compass Thine altar.' The psalmist felt that unless there was a previous lustration and cleansing, it was vain for him to go round the altar. And you may remember how sternly and eloquently the prophet Isaiah rebukes the hypocritical worshippers in Jerusalem when he says to them, 'Your hands are full of blood. Wash you, make you clean; put away the evil of your doings,' and then come and pray. A foul hand gets nothing from God. How can it? God's best gift is of such a sort as cannot be laid upon a dirty palm. A little sin dams back the whole of God's grace, and there are too many men that pray, pray, pray, and never get any of the things that we pray for, because there is something stopping the pipe, and they do not know what it is and perhaps would be very sorry to clear it out if they did."[170]

Therefore the lifting up of "clean hands" and "holy hands" essentially meant the heart was free from sinful contamination that would interfere with proper praying and worship. Albert Barnes summarizes the practice in saying, "The idea is that when men approach God, they should do it in a pure and holy manner."[171] With that assessment John Gill agrees, stating the lifting up of holy hands unto the Lord is "an emblem of the elevation of the heart in prayer to God, without which the former would be of little avail."[172]

The Bottom Line: The uplifting of the hand in prayer and worship is hypocritical if the heart is impure. The practice is commended but not commanded in Holy Scripture. The uplifted hand symbolizes purity of heart and signifies expectation for God's speedy answer.

Chapter 21

Hurry Jeopardizes Prayer

"We can slight our praying and not realize the peril till the foundations are gone. Hurried devotions make weak faith, feeble convictions, questionable piety."[173] ~ E. M. Bounds

Samuel Chadwick wrote, "Hurry is the death of prayer."[174] Our Lord says, "Be still, and know that I am God" (Psalm 46:10). Prayer mustn't be rushed or hurried, except in dire circumstances demanding it be so—like when Peter was drowning (Matthew 14:30). Plan the day around prayer, not prayer around the day, that it be calmly and unhurriedly engaged in. Stephen Olford wrote, "Five minutes in quiet waiting upon God will yield far more than thirty hurried minutes."[175] "Wait calmly for God alone, my soul, because my hope comes from him" (Psalm 62:5 GW).

A beggar knocked upon a house door requesting food. The lady, in seeing him, quickly ran to the kitchen to get him something to eat. The man waited a moment, then turned to walk away. Seeing him depart, the woman called for his return. He almost missed a good meal for failure to wait. Only God knows how many "good meals" (provision, supply, blessing, gifts) we have missed by failure "to wait" at His door. Don't be in a rush when you knock at God's door. Saith Gordon Watt, "Let us guard against rush in the prayer life, against the device of the enemy to drive and push us either to act without prayer, or pray without quietness of spirit."[176]

Chapter 22

Pray Specifically

"Prayer is not putting your hand into a bag and pulling out what comes first. Oh, no; there must be definite desires and specific requests."[177] ~ C. H. Spurgeon

Advises Andrew Murray, "Pray with definite requests."[178] Saith Gordon Watt, "Indefiniteness of language is as ineffective on the knees in the prayer room as on the feet in the pulpit. [It] calls for definiteness and directness of petition."[179] With regard to prayer, "generalities do not pierce deep enough,"[180] and "dealing in generalities is the death of prayer."[181] "Requests" (Philippians 4:6) refer to specific things asked for, as does 'petition' in Ephesians 6:18. Praying specifically enables you to connect that which was requested with God's answer, thus strengthening confidence in prayer and glorifying God.

Spurgeon remarked, "There is a general kind of praying which fails for lack of precision. It is as if a regiment of soldiers should all fire off their guns anywhere. Possibly somebody would be killed, but the majority of the enemy would be missed."[182] Spurgeon further advised, "When you pray, tell Him what you want. If you don't have enough money, if you are in poverty, if you are in desperate need, state the case. Don't be shy with God. Come at once to the point; speak honestly with Him."[183]

And do the same with requests for others. Avoid the overused, worn-out phrase, "Bless so and so." Expressly tell the Lord what you would like Him to do in their behalf. Adam Clarke suggests, "Make your requests earnestly and specifically if you desire definite answers. It is the aimlessness of prayer that accounts for so many seemingly unanswered prayers. Fill your check out for something definite, and it will be cashed at the bank of Heaven."[184]

Two blind men heard that Jesus was passing by. They cried out, 'Lord, have mercy on us.'

Jesus asked, 'What do you want me to do for you?'

They said, 'Lord, we want our eyes opened. We want to see!' Only then did Jesus touch their eyes, healing their sight (Matthew 20:29–34).

Avoid vagueness in prayer. Be specific in making requests. Although the two blind men were persistent in prayer (they cried out for help so much the crowd told them to quieten down), exhibited faith in prayer (they cried, 'O Lord, Son of David'), it wasn't until they specifically told Jesus what they wanted Him to do that their prayer was answered. As you pray, hear Him ask of you, 'What do you want me to do for you?' (Matthew 20:32). And then answer frankly and pointedly.

Chapter 23

Don't Give Up Until God Answers

"The great fault of the children of God is, they do not continue in prayer; they do not go on praying; they do not persevere. If they desire anything for God's glory, they should pray until they get it."[185] ~ George Müller

"The most difficult prayer," wrote Ole Hallesby, "and the prayer which, therefore, costs us the most striving, is persevering prayer, the prayer which faints not but continues steadfastly until the answer comes."[186] "Will not God make the things that are right come to His chosen people who cry day and night to Him?" (Luke 18:7 NLV). Daniel prayed three full weeks about a matter before receiving the answer of God (Daniel 10:2). Persist in prayer until prompted by the Holy Spirit to desist, as was the case with Paul (2 Corinthians 12:8–9). Travail, travail, travail until you prevail, prevail, prevail. "Importunate praying," says E. M. Bounds, "has patience to wait and strength to continue. It never prepares itself to quit praying and declines to rise from its knees until an answer is received."[187] Jim Cymbala said, "Persistent calling upon the name of the Lord breaks through every stronghold of the Devil, for nothing is impossible with God."[188] To waver in faith is to hinder answer to prayer. Don't allow delay in answer to prayer to dictate belief. Despite the direction the winds blow, be unshakeable in your confidence (faith) that God will answer the prayer based upon His Word and Sovereign will (James 1:6–7).

Saith Samuel Chadwick, "There is no power like that of prevailing prayer; of Abraham pleading for Sodom; of Jacob wrestling in the stillness of the night; of Moses standing in the breach; of Hannah intoxicated with sorrow; of David heartbroken with remorse and grief; of Jesus sweating, as it were, great drops of blood. Such prayer prevails. It turns ordinary mortals into men of power. It brings power, fire, and rain. It brings life because it brings God."[189] Let us, therefore, prevail in prayer. Prevail in prayer against the strongholds of Satan, areas wherein Satan is blocking or hindering God's work. Prevail in prayer for souls in satanic bondage and darkness. Prevail in prayer for church revival and national awakening. Prevail in prayer for personal and ministry needs. Prevail in prayer until evil is replaced with the rule of good. Prevail in prayer for friends and family battling illness, temptation, trial, and trouble. Prevail in prayer for the widow and widower and orphan. Prevail in prayer for the persecuted church. Prevail in prayer for laborers to be thrust into the harvest. See Colossians 4:12–13.

How long should we persevere in prayer about a matter? Until it is answered or we get assurance that it will be answered or God prompts us to stop. Saith Jon Courson: "Pray three times, thirty times, three hundred times until you either get the answer you're asking for or you hear the Father say, 'No, and here's why not.' Don't settle for anything less. Talk to the Father about your thorns, your difficulties, and keep praying until the answer comes your way or until, like Paul, you have understanding and revelation and can say, 'That's a closed issue. I don't need to talk about that anymore. I get it, Father. Your grace is sufficient for me.'"[190] George Müller testified, "Tens of thousands of times my prayers have been answered. When once I am persuaded a thing is right, I go on praying for it until the end comes. I never give up!"[191]

The faith-based biblical prayer of the saints uttered in purity of heart for the glory of God, though delayed or modified, will be answered. And the answer, J. I. Packer says, will be a huge "positive, though it may be 'I am adjusting the terms of your prayer to give you something better than you asked for.' Or it may be, 'I know that this isn't the moment in which answering your prayer would bring you and others most blessing, so I'm asking you to wait.' Or it may be, 'I am answering your prayer, but you don't know the strategy I'm working on, and it doesn't at the moment feel or look like an answer at all. Nonetheless, it is. Keep praying, keep trusting, and keep looking for what, down the road, I may be able in wisdom to let you see.'"[192] Testified Spurgeon: "In the name of Jesus, I have asked and received, *except* only when I have asked amiss. It is true I have had to wait because my time was ill-judged and God's time was far better, but delays are not denials."[193] "The secret of prevailing prayer," writes Wesley Duewel, "is simply to pray until the answer comes. The length of time is ultimately immaterial. It is God's answer that counts. The length of time required may often seem perplexing and may prove a test of your faith."[194]

To underscore the importance of praying with importunity (relentlessly and persistently), Jesus shared the parable of the importunate widow (Luke 18:1–8). A widow pleaded with a judge for help. Being denied, she pleaded again and again. Finally, the judge said, "'I fear neither God nor man…but this woman bothers me. I'm going to see that she gets justice, for she is wearing me out with her constant coming!' Then the Lord said, 'If even an evil judge can be worn down like that, don't you think that God will surely give justice to his people who plead with him day and night? Yes! He will answer them quickly!'" (Luke 18:5–8 TLB). The lesson: God wants us to pray, pray, and keep praying until that which is His will is granted. "There is always an open ear if you have an open mouth. There is always a ready hand if you have a ready heart. You have but to cry, and the Lord hears; nay, before you call, He will answer; and while you are speaking, He will hear. Oh! be not backward then in prayer."[195]

Knock persistently and expectantly upon the door to the throne of grace. But then patiently await an answer. A minister, often interrupted by annoying knocks on his door by fleeing children, hung under the knocker the polite request, "Please don't knock unless you wait for an answer." "To pray and not to look for an answer argues either a mere formality in prayer, and that makes the prayer to be dead; or else unbelief as to the truth of God, and that makes the prayer to be corrupt. How many runaway knocks we give at mercy's gate! Let us put away such childish things and treat prayer as a reality; then shall we be answered of a truth."[196] Let's not knock at the door to the throne of grace unless we're willing to wait for God to answer.[197] In due time, He will, if we faint not. "Knock, and it shall be opened unto you" (Matthew 7:7).

Thomas Manton wrote, "A good dog hunts by sight as long as he can see his game; but when that is lost, he hunts by scent." Spurgeon makes application of the saying to prayer: "So in prayer we are to pursue the blessing while we are encouraged to seek it, but we are not to cease when the likelihood of success is gone. We must hunt by a spiritual scent when sight quite fails us. The odor of the promise must direct our way when the mercy is numbered with the 'things not seen as yet.'"[198]

Chapter 24

Pray About Everything

"Prayer is for every moment of our lives, not just for times of suffering or joy."[199] ~ Billy Graham

Helmut Thielicke, a German theologian, points out that the petitions of the "Lord's Prayer" (Matthew 6) are all-comprehensive. "Great things, small things, spiritual things and material things, inward things and outward things—there is nothing that is not included in this prayer."[200] The point? "There's nothing in life outside the reach of prayer."[201] With God nothing is impossible (Luke 1:37). "Prayer can change anything. The impossible doesn't exist. His is the power. Ours is the prayer."[202] Saith Oswald Chambers, "We tend to use prayer as a last resort, but God wants it to be our first line of defense. We pray when there's nothing else we can do, but God wants us to pray before we do anything at all."[203] Let's be careful not to limit the Holy One of Israel (Psalm 78:41) by failure to bring everything to Him in prayer. God is generous and loving to His children. He gives loaves of bread, not baskets of stones (Matthew 7:7–11) in response to their cry for help. "There is no bottom to His treasuries. He is the true Solomon, and His daily provision is not only enough for all His household, but for all those who lie starving on the highways and in the hedges. The wealth of nations is nothing to the wealth of Jesus. Come, then, my heart; beg largely of thy Lord, and when He hears thee, beg again."[204]

Adrian Rogers said, "Can I pray about small things? A parking space? 'That's silly; that's too small.' Can you think of anything that's 'big' to God? Nothing is 'big' to God. Things are neither big nor small to Him. The biggest thing you can think of is small to God, and the smallest thing you can think of is important to God...if it's important to you. If it concerns you, it concerns God."[205] See Psalm 78:41. Prayer is to be all inclusive. Billy Graham states, "We are to pray in times of adversity, lest we become faithless and unbelieving. We are to pray in times of prosperity, lest we become boastful and proud. We are to pray in times of danger, lest we become fearful and doubting. We are to pray in times of security, lest we become self-sufficient."[206]

A young, devout Christian German boy sought to always be on time at school, as the headmaster instructed. One morning as he left for school, the clock struck the time he was to be there. As he walked to the school, he prayed aloud, "O Lord, don't let me be late for school." A man overheard the prayer and thought it a foolish request and out of curiosity followed the boy to the school just to see what would happen. Surprisingly, the boy arrived just as the headmaster and other students walked in the door of the school. He arrived on time! You see, the headmaster had a problem unlocking the door and had to call for a locksmith to resolve the matter.[207] Coincidental? Don't believe it for a minute. "This is the finger of God"

(Exodus 8:19) at work in response to the prayer and faith of a young boy. Let the story remind the believer that even the smallest of things are important to God and worthy of prayer. Don't limit God (Psalm 78:41).

> What a Friend we have in Jesus,
>> All our sins and griefs to bear!
> What a privilege to carry
>> Everything to God in prayer!
>
> Oh, what peace we often forfeit;
>> Oh, what needless pain we bear,
> All because we do not carry
>> Everything to God in prayer!
>
> ~ Joseph Scriven (1855)

Yes, pray about everything. But don't ask for just anything. Requests to God are restricted. Warren Wiersbe says, "We have no right to ask God for anything that will dishonor His name, delay His kingdom, or disturb His will on earth."[208]

Chapter 25

Principle of Glancing and Gazing

"We have to pray with our eyes on God, not on the difficulties."[209] ~ Oswald Chambers

Glance at the need; *gaze* upon God. Jesus appeared to the disciples walking on the water toward their boat (Matthew 14:25). Impetuous Peter asked permission to go to Him. But Peter's calm prayer quickly turned to one of panic when he began to gaze at the waves and water about him instead of looking to Jesus. "Beginning to sink," he cried out in panic, "Lord, save me" (Matthew 14:30). As long as Peter fixed his gaze on Jesus, only glancing at the water and waves, he successfully walked on the water of the Sea of Galilee. Facing the storms of life, glance at the difficulty, but then in faith steadfastly gaze or focus upon Christ in prayer, who hath the power to still the waves with the words "peace, be still" (Mark 4:39). It's when the principle is reversed that we panic and begin to "sink."

Chapter 26

Fervency in Prayer

"Prayers must be red hot. It is the fervent prayer that is effectual and that availeth. Coldness of spirit hinders praying; prayer cannot live in a wintry atmosphere."[210] ~ E. M. Bounds

Prayer that is power filled is not listless or cold, but passionate. James says, "The effectual fervent prayer of a righteous man availeth much" (James 5:16). Powerful praying is passionate, earnest, hearty, sincere praying.[211] Spurgeon advises about praying, "One warm, hearty prayer is worth twenty of those packed in ice."[212] An old divine said that fervent prayer "is like a cannon planted at the gates of Heaven; it makes them fly open."[213] Samuel Chadwick comments, "The prayer that prevails is not the work of lips and fingertips. It is the cry of a broken heart and the travail of a stricken soul."[214] J. C. Ryle said, "Words said without heart are as utterly useless to our souls as the drumbeating of savages before their idols. Where there is no heart, there may be lip work and tongue work, but there is no prayer."[215] "Cold prayers," says an aged Christian, "ask for a denial."[216] Thomas Brooks wrote, "Cold prayers shall never have any warm answers."[217]

Saith Bounds, "No erudition, no purity of diction, no width of mental outlook, no flowers of eloquence, no grace of person can atone for lack of fire. Prayer ascends by fire. Flame gives prayer access as well as wings, acceptance as well as energy. There is no incense without fire, no prayer without flame."[218]

I often say my prayers;
　　But do I ever pray?
And do the wishes of my heart
　　Go with the words I say?

I may as well kneel down
　　And worship gods of stone
As offer to the living God
　　A prayer of words alone.

For words without the heart
　　The Lord will never hear,
Nor will he to those lips attend
　　Whose prayers are not sincere.

~ John Burton (1803–1877)

Prayer fervency is not synonymous with praying loudly, raising the hands in prayer, walking around in prayer, or praying out loud with others simultaneously. Rather, it is characterized by the heart crying out to God energetically, passionately, and earnestly about that which is requested at His hand (James 5:16). Whence doth this fervency in prayer come? Saith E. M. Bounds, "It's not in our power, perhaps, to create fervency of spirit at will, but we can pray God to implant it. It is ours then, to nourish and cherish it, to guard it against extinction, to prevent its abatement or decline."[219]

Epaphras prayed fervently. Saith Paul, "Epaphras, who is one of you, a servant of Christ Jesus, saluteth you, always striving [to struggle, fight, wrestle] for you in his prayers, that ye may stand perfect and fully assured in all the will of God. For I bear him witness, that he hath much labor for you, and for them in Laodicea" (Colossians 4:12–13 ASV). The Greek word for "striving" pictures a man toiling at work until utterly weary (Colossians 1:29), an athlete competing in a contest with fixed purpose to win (1 Corinthians 9:25), and a soldier fighting or battling to save his life (1 Timothy 6:12).[220] Jon

Courson states the idea is of one giving birth, travailing in pain to give birth to prayer (shrugging and fighting off hindrances to praying) and laboring in prayer until there is a break-through.[221] Epaphras *toiled, agonized, battled* and *travailed* in prayer for the saints at Colossae and Laodicea. See Genesis 32:28 for Jacob's prayer. Samuel Chadwick says, "Intensity is a law of prayer. God is found by those who seek Him with all their heart. Wrestling prayer prevails. The fervent effectual prayer of the righteous is of great force."[222] We know not if Epaphras was a great orator of the Gospel, but he certainly was a man of great prayer (which is by far the better).

Matthew Henry says, "Those who would succeed in prayer [like Epaphras] must take pains in prayer; and we must be earnest in prayer, not only for ourselves, but for others also."[223] "There is travail in it. There is work in it. There is entreaty in it. There is importunity in it."[224] Like Epaphras, let us labor in prayer consistently, relentlessly, and fervently in behalf of another person or a cause for the known will of God until it is accomplished. But, William Booth cautions, "This kind of prayer be sure the Devil and the world and your own indolent, unbelieving nature will oppose."[225]

> We do not forget to eat; we do not forget to be diligent in business; we do not forget to go to our beds to rest; but we often do forget to wrestle with God in prayer and to spend, as we ought to spend, long periods in consecrated fellowship with our Father and our God.
> ~ C. H. Spurgeon [*Prayers from Metropolitan Pulpit: C. H. Spurgeon's Prayers.* (New York: Revell, 1906), 139.]

Bear in mind that the wrestling in prayer that Epaphras did was not the kind that sought to manipulate God's will or force Him to action. As Ole Hallesby says, "It is not necessary for us to pray or wrestle in prayer in order to make God kind or generous. He is not only good; He is also omniscient, knowing at all times what is best for us. It is not necessary for us to try to teach Him what is best for us by argumentation, persuasion, or much talking (James 1:5)."[226] Rather, Epaphras' wrestling was that of exhibiting persistency and fervency in prayer for that to be done which was known to be the will of God. To wrestle otherwise, contrary to the will of God and His revealed Word, is to pray amiss, and therefore futilely.

Chapter 27

Pray with Expectation

"To pray without expectation is to misunderstand the whole concept of prayer and relationship with God."[227]

~ A. W. Tozer

Alexander Maclaren describes the strength of faith: "A cupful of water poured into a hydraulic ram sets in motion power that lifts tons; the prayer of faith brings the dread magnificence of Jehovah into the field."[228] Confidence (faith) in prayer is to say, "I am sure that I shall receive either what I ask or what I should ask."[229] How apt we are to pray dubiously, to pray as if God did not mean what He said or cannot be trusted to do as asked. L. B. Cowman wrote, "Genuine faith puts its letter in the mailbox and lets go. Distrust, however, holds on to a corner of the envelope and then wonders why the answer never arrives."[230] In praying, it's often distrust or unbelief that keeps the answer at bay (Matthew 21:22). Great prayers require great faith! Effective prayer is founded on faith, a confident expectation in Christ's ability and willingness to do that which is asked.

Prayer, as Jerry Bridges suggests, "is the most tangible expression of trust in God."[231] "It's impossible to please God apart from faith. And why? Because anyone who wants to approach God must believe both that he exists and that he cares enough to respond to those who seek him" (Hebrews 11:6 MSG). James O. Fraser, missionary to China in the early twentieth century, said, "Praying without faith is like trying to cut with a blunt knife—much labor expended to little purpose."[232] Dietrich Bonhoeffer states, "It matters little what form of prayer we adopt or how many words we use. What matters is the faith which lays hold on God, knowing that He knows our needs before we even ask Him. That is what gives Christian prayer its boundless confidence and its joyous certainty."[233] Nothing will stir us to mighty prayer as much as telling ourselves while in prayer that God is really going to do that which is requested.[234] Adrian Rogers said, "It is not the eloquence and form of our prayers that gets them delivered, but the stamp of faith. Like they say, 'Pray, believe, and you'll receive. Pray and doubt; you'll do without.'"[235]

George Müller was aboard ship en route to Quebec for a speaking engagement when a dense fog threatened a late arrival and cancellation of the service. When the ship's captain was invited to pray with him in the chartroom about the matter, he said to Müller, "Do you realize how dense the fog is?" "No," he replied, "my eye is not on the dense fog but on the living God who controls every circumstance of my life." Müller prayed for the fog to lift in five minutes. It did, and his engagement was made possible.[236] He prayed in faith with expectation and was not disappointed.

Faith in prayer is fueled by its Worker. It's not confidence in the act of prayer but in an omnipotent God to whom it is uttered and who is capable of answering that makes faith strong and bold. This God declares, "I am the LORD, the God of all people. Nothing is too difficult for me" (Jeremiah 32:27 GNT) and "Open thy mouth wide, and I will fill it" (Psalm 81:10). E. M. Bounds says, "The faith which creates powerful praying is the faith which centers itself on a powerful Person. Faith in Christ's ability to do and to do greatly is the faith which prays greatly."[237] Spurgeon said, "Know more of Christ, think more of Him, and your faith will increase. Your little faith would soon get strong if you lived more on Jesus."[238]

Faith in prayer is fueled by its Work. The psalmist declared, "I will remember the works of the LORD. Yes, I will remember the amazing things you did long ago. I will think about all you have done; I will reflect upon your deeds. O God, your deeds are extraordinary" (Psalms 77:11–13 NET). Remembering God's wonders and miracles of old in response to the cries of His people builds faith. James McConkey says, "The hound [saint] that hath a sure trail [numerous answered prayers] runs with confidence, while his doubting companion stands baying aloft in disappointed perplexity."[239]

Faith in prayer is fueled by its Witness. Eyewitness testimonies about the efficacy of prayer builds faith. Hear and read the accounts of people that experienced first-hand answer to prayer. Saith Spurgeon, "The very best way to put to rout the falsehood of philosophic atheists [about prayer] is more real prayer; facts are unanswerable."[240]

Faith in prayer is fueled by its Word. Paul declared, "Faith cometh by hearing, and hearing by the word of God" (Romans 10:17). Scripture time and again speaks of the divine authorization of prayer as the means to acquire that which is needed or desired. Jesus said, "Therefore I say unto you, what things soever ye desire, when ye pray, believe that ye receive them, and ye shall have them" (Mark 11:24), and, "Ask, and it shall be given you; seek, and ye shall find; knock, and it shall be opened unto you: For every one that asketh receiveth; and he that seeketh findeth; and to him that knocketh it shall be opened" (Matthew 7:7–8), and, "This is the confidence that we have in Him, that, if we ask anything according to His will, He heareth us" (1 John 5:14). These declarations are the word of Him that is incapable of lying (Titus 1:2; Hebrews 6:18). Spurgeon said, "When a person really prays, it is not a question whether God will hear them or not; He must hear them—not because there is any compulsion in the prayer, but there is a sweet and blessed compulsion in the promise. God has promised to hear prayer, and He will keep His promise."[241] Further,

Spurgeon said, "Ye shall ask; ye shall always ask. Ye shall never get beyond asking, but ye shall ask successfully, for 'ye shall ask what ye will, and it shall be done unto you.'"[242]

Come, ye who from your hearts believe
    That Jesus answers prayer;
Come boldly to a throne of grace
    And claim His promise there

That, if His love in us abide
    And we in Him are one,
Whatever in His Name we ask,
    It surely will be done.

Come lovingly and trustingly;
    Take Jesus at His Word,
For He has said, "The prayer of faith
    Was never yet unheard." ~ Fanny Crosby

Chapter 28

Prayer Blockers

"God has not placed Himself under obligation to honor the requests of worldly, carnal or disobedient Christians. He hears and answers the prayers only of those who walk in His way."[243] ~ A. W. Tozer

"So that your prayers may not be hindered" (1 Peter 3:7 ESV). John R. Rice said, "The normal Christian life is a life of regular, daily answer to prayer. In the model prayer, Jesus taught His disciples to pray daily for bread and expect to get it, and to ask daily for forgiveness, for deliverance from the evil one, and for other needs, and daily to get the answers they sought."[244] If this be so, and it is, then why is it that Christians at times pray for that which is God's will and do not get an answer to their prayers. The answer is revealed by Isaiah. "Behold, the LORD'S hand is not shortened, that it cannot save; neither his ear heavy, that it cannot hear: but your iniquities have separated between you and your God, and your sins have hid his face from you, that he will not hear" (Isaiah 59:1–2). Sin blocks prayer from being effective. As John Blanchard states, "We cannot expect to live defectively and pray effectively."[245] Matthew Henry states, "The hands must be cleansed by faith, repentance, and reformation, or it will be in vain for us to draw nigh to God in prayer or in any of the exercises of devotion."[246]

God has not left us in the dark with regard to the sins that hinder prayer, having enumerated them clearly in Scripture. They include: disobedience (Micah 3:4; Deuteronomy 1:43–45; Jeremiah 11:10–11); arrogance (James 4:6–10; Job 35:12–13); hypocrisy (Mark 12:38–40; Matthew 15:1–9); refusal to help the poor (Proverbs 21:13); unconfessed sin (John 9:31; Isaiah 59:1–2; Psalm 66:18); unforgiving spirit (Mark 11:25); indifference toward the Word of God (Proverbs 28:9); wrong relationship with husband or wife (1 Peter 3:7); delinquent debts (Matthew 5:23–24; Luke 19:8); selfishness (James 4:3); lack of faith (James 1:6–7); and praying outside God's will (Luke 22:42). If we are imprisoned in the cage of any of these sins, unresponsive to God's authority, the windows of Heaven remain closed to our prayers. When we submit to the Lordship of Christ, Heaven's windows of bounty open and empty out freely that which is requested in accordance with God's will.

Answered prayer will come to him that may say truthfully,

Nothing between my soul and the Savior,
    So that His blessed face may be seen;
Nothing preventing the least of His favor,
    Keep the way clear—let nothing between.
                ~ Charles Albert Tindley (1905)

An employee who worked for a city located in a valley was fired. In anger, he plugged the primary pipe that supplied water to the city from the reservoir in the mountain. The flow of the water to the city halted. Efforts to ascertain the cause were unsuccessful. The distraught employee finally owned up to the deed. Upon removal of the plug, the water flowed freely again.

Answers to prayer will flow fluidly and freely for the believer who through confession and repentance removes from the pipe the plug that is hindering prayer (1 John 1:9).

Chapter 29

Divine Prompting to Pray

"The Holy Spirit is active in 1) bringing to mind people or circumstances we ought to pray for, and 2) giving rise to prayer that exactly the mark hits."[247] ~ Jack Hayford

"One of the most subtle burdens God ever puts on us as saints," says Oswald Chambers, "is this burden of discernment concerning other souls. He reveals things in order that we may take the burden of these souls before Him."[248] Discernment or divine prompting comes by way of the Holy Spirit and is like a lightning flash out of nowhere bringing to mind a person, ministry, circumstance, or event for which to pray. When so prompted (Spurgeon says, "Let a hint from the Holy Spirit be enough for thee"[249]) stop what you're doing and pray then and there. Never postpone the prayer for what you count a better time or place. Martyn Lloyd-Jones advises, "Always respond to every impulse to pray. I would make an absolute law of this: always obey such an impulse."[250] Charles Finney said, "If you find yourself drawn out in mighty prayer for certain individuals, exercised with great compassion, agonized with strong crying and tears for a certain family or neighborhood or people, let such an influence be yielded to."[251]

Sensitivity to the Spirit's prompting to pray comes with experience. The more the Spirit's impulse to pray is heeded, the more sensitive one is to it.

Chapter 30

Getting Past the Hindrances

"Satan cannot deny but that great wonders have been wrought by prayer. As the spirit of prayer goes up, so his kingdom goes down. Satan's strategies against prayer are three. First, if he can, he will keep thee from prayer. If that be not feasible, secondly, he will strive to interrupt thee in prayer. And, thirdly, if that plot takes not, he will labor to hinder the success of thy prayer."[252] ~ William Gurnall

"But Satan hindered us" (1 Thessalonians 2:18).

Hindrances *to* prayer.

Saith Ole Hallesby, "That our wrestling is not against flesh and blood, but against the spiritual hosts of wickedness in the heavenly places (Ephesians 6:12), we see plainly when we begin to take notice of the outward hindrances which are placed in the way of our prayers from day to day. When those hours of the day come in which we should be having our prayer sessions with God, it often appears as though everything has entered into a conspiracy to prevent it—human beings, animals, and, above all, the telephone. It is not difficult to see that there is a veiled hand in the complot."[253] Similarly, David Wilkerson wrote, "If you set your heart to seek God, the Devil will put on you a conspiracy of interruptions. He will do all he can to keep you from the prayer closet." Andrew Bonar writes, "The Prince of the power of the air seems to bend all the force of his attack against the spirit of prayer."[254] Mary Booth, the wife of William Booth, said, "Depend upon it; if you are bent on prayer, the Devil will not leave you alone. He will molest you, tantalize you, block you, and will surely find some hindrances, big or little or both.

And we sometimes fail because we are ignorant of his devices."[255] J. C. Ryle said, "Do we ever feel a secret inclination...to become careless about our prayers or omit our prayers altogether? Let us be sure, when we do, that it is a direct temptation from the Devil. He is trying to sap and undermine the very citadel of our souls."[256] Despite Satan's effort to distract from and deter prayer, pray. "If the enemy can distract you from your time alone with God, then he can isolate you from the help that comes from God alone."[257]

Hindrances *in* prayer.

As a runner, occasionally I encounter what is called a "runner's wall," a point of resistance that must be vigorously challenged to proceed. The man that prays will face such walls and must push himself past them with the help of the Holy Spirit. Paul says, "Strive...in your prayers" (Romans 15:30). That is, let us, as Ole Hallesby states, "struggle through those hindrances which would restrain or even prevent us entirely from continuing in persevering prayer."[258] Prayer will not always be borne along with freedom and joy. It wasn't for Hudson Taylor, who testified: "'Sometimes I pray on with my heart feeling like wood.' Then he added, 'Often, too, the most wonderful answers have come when prayer has been a real effort of faith, without any joy whatever.'"[259]

Spurgeon advises, "Not to pray because you do not feel fit to pray is like saying, 'I will not take medicine because I am too ill.' Pray for prayer; pray yourself, by the Spirit's assistance, into a praying frame."[260] Pray when you feel like it. When you don't feel like praying, pray until you do feel like it. When prayer is the hardest thing to do, pray the hardest. With the help of the Holy Spirit, pray through the wall of hindrance. "Resist the devil, and he will flee from you" (James 4:7). Further Spurgeon states,

"When you feel disinclined to pray, let it be a sign to you that prayer is doubly necessary! Pray for prayer!"[261]

Saith Ole Hallesby, "To move in prayer as though one were in one's element; to pray daily with a willing spirit, with joy, with gratitude, and with adoration is something which is far beyond our human capacities and abilities. A miracle of God is necessary every day for this. This miracle consists in receiving the Spirit of prayer."[262]

Chapter 31

Saying, "Amen"

"I could wish that we more uniformly and universally said Amen at the close of public prayer; I am sure it would be scriptural and apostolic, and I believe it would be useful to you all."[263] ~ C. H. Spurgeon

The word "Amen" at the conclusion of prayer denotes, "So be it; so let it be." Martin Luther said, "'Amen' meaneth 'assuredly'; namely, that I am sure that petitions of this kind are accepted by my Heavenly Father and heard by Him, because He hath commanded us that we should pray after this manner and hath promised that He will hear us. Amen, Amen; that is, truly, certainly, so be it."[264]

Spurgeon states, "Amen is what we may call petitionary. In this sense we use it at the close of our prayers. 'Our Father who art in heaven' is not a complete model of public prayer till it concludes with 'Amen.' In the ancient Church it was customary for the entire congregation to say Amen."[265] Paul references the practice as occurring in the Corinthian church (1 Corinthians 14:16), as doth Jerome with the saints in Rome in his day. Despite seeing the Amen in some assemblies "put in the wrong place," which thereby "rather created ridicule than reverence and showed as much folly as fervor," Spurgeon believed a judicious revival of its custom would be useful to the church.[266]

> Let every creature rise and bring
> Peculiar honors to our King.
> Angels, descend with songs again;
> And earth, repeat the long AMEN.
>
> ~ Isaac Watts (1674–1748)

Say "Amen" to personal prayers and to those of others if you are in hearty agreement with that which was said. But do so with meaning. A. W. Tozer cautions, "Such words as *amen, hallelujah, glory,* and others of like sacred association are repeated endlessly and meaninglessly in the apparent belief that they have in them some strange power for good. This can be no more than high-grade magic. It will pay us to search our own hearts thoroughly to discover just why we use these words."[267]

Note: The word also may be used outside of the context of prayer to give consent or agreement to that which the minister, musician, testifier, or teacher proclaims.

PART THREE
Forms of Prayer

Chapter 32

Praying Alone

"The one place where the Lord's presence and power will be more fully realized than any other place is the closet of prayer."[268] ~ E. M. Bounds

It is to the closet Christ tells us to go to pray: "But when you pray, go into your most private room, close the door and pray to your Father who is in secret, and your Father who sees…in secret will reward you" (Matthew 6:6 AMP). It's in the private, secret closet with the door shut to the distractions and disruptions of the world and to the ears of others that the saint voices the sincerest and most ardent prayer. Regarding the bliss of solitude (closet praying), Andrew Murray wrote, "Oh, the thought of having God all alone to myself and knowing that God has me all alone to Himself!"[269] How totally awesome is that! Saith Spurgeon, "Secret religion is the very soul of godliness. What we are alone, that alone we are. Private communion with Jesus is a better sign of grace than all the outward sacraments that were ever attended."[270]

Jesus practiced closet praying (Luke 5:16), as did Elijah under a juniper tree (1 Kings 19:4), Jeremiah in a deep miry pit (Lamentations 3:55–57), Daniel in the roof chamber of his house (Daniel 6:10), Hezekiah on a sickbed (2 Kings 20:2), Jonah in a fish's belly (Jonah 2:1), and Peter on a rooftop (Acts 10:9). It's the privacy of prayer, not its place, that is all important. Matthew Henry comments, "Secret prayer is to be performed in retirement, that we may be unobserved and so may avoid ostentation, undisturbed and so may avoid distraction, unheard and so may use greater freedom."[271] And to the minister specifically Spurgeon said, "All our libraries and studies are mere emptiness compared to our closets. We grow, we wax mighty, we prevail in private prayer."[272] Seth Joshua wrote, "All prayer is hidden. It is behind a closed door. The best spade diggers go down into deep ditches out of sight. There are numbers of surface workers, but few who in self-obliteration toil alone with God."[273]

John Calvin remarks, "It is useful to pray apart, for then the faithful soul develops itself more familiarly and with greater simplicity pours forth its petitions, groans, cares, fears, hopes, and joys into the bosom of God."[274] James emphasizes the power of praying alone in saying, "The earnest prayer of a righteous man [one man] has great power and wonderful results" (James 5:16 TLB). Closet praying (any secluded place free from the view of man and distraction) provides privacy for secret sins, secret desires, and secret temptations to be expressed. It is less mingled with pride, hypocrisy, and the desire to impress another in its utterance.

It guards against false motives in praying. R. C. Sproul says one might preach out of false motives and do Christian work out of false motives, but it is highly unlikely he will pray with false motives when praying privately.[275] Closet prayer, aloneness with God, promotes personal intimacy with Him (James 4:8). "The more you are on your knees alone, the better."[276] Thomas à Kempis well said, "You will find in your 'closet of prayer' what you frequently lose when you are out in the world. The more you visit it, the more you will want to return. If you are faithful to your secret place, it will become your closest friend and bring you much comfort. The tears shed there bring cleansing."[277]

> I have a house inside of me,
> A house that people never see.
> It has a door through which none pass,
> And windows, but they're not of glass.

I meet my heavenly Father there,
For He stoops down to hear my prayer,
To heal my wounds and cure my care,
And make me strong to do and dare.

Then after I am made quite strong
And things are right that were all wrong,
I go outside where I belong
And sing a new and happy song.

You have a house inside of you,
Where you can fight your battles through,
And God will tell you what to do
And make your heart both strong and true.[278]

~ S. W. Graflin

Saith Matthew Henry, "If we cannot go to the house of the Lord, we can go by faith to the Lord of the house."[279]

Chapter 33

Praying with Others

"By praying with friends, you will be able to hear and see facets of Jesus that you have not yet perceived."[280]

~ Tim Keller

Prior to Pentecost the apostles and others engaged in a prayer meeting: "Peter, and James, and John, and Andrew, Philip, and Thomas, Bartholomew, and Matthew, James the son of Alphaeus, and Simon Zelotes, and Judas the brother of James. These all continued with one accord in prayer and supplication, with the women, and Mary the mother of Jesus, and with his brethren" (Acts 1:13–14). This explains the powerful effect of Peter's preaching on the day of Pentecost and that of the testimonies of others that resulted in 3,000 converts! Members of the early church were devoted to praying together (Acts 2:42). Upon being released from prison, the disciples met for united prayer (Acts 4:31). Lydia and other believers met at a riverside to pray regularly (Acts 16:13–14). The people united with Nehemiah to pray when rebuilding the walls of Jerusalem (Nehemiah 1:11). Daniel requested Shadrach, Meshach, and Abednego to pray specifically for God to grant him understanding of the king's dream (Daniel 2:17–18). That prayer meeting of four in the home of Daniel reveals the power of united prayer. "Then," that is, following their prayer, "was the secret revealed unto Daniel in a night vision" (Daniel 2:19). Oh, the impact of joint prayer!

John of Kronstadt said, "I reverence even two or three praying together, for in accordance with the Lord's promise, He Himself is in the midst of them (Matthew 18:20)."[281] Charles Finney states, "Nothing tends more to cement the hearts of Christians than praying together. Never do they love one another so well as when they witness the outpouring of each other's hearts in prayer."[282] Wesley Duewel said, "Prayer is the supreme way to be workers together with God."[283] Joint praying elevates faith in God's promises and power through believers' witnessing of its miraculous results together. In joint praying the stronger believer's faith undergirds and bolsters the weaker believer. Joint prayer binds hearts in agreement on that which is requested, making the answer more likely (Matthew 18:20).

Joint prayer "shakes" problems, places, and people. Scripture states that when the disciples were released from prison they prayed, and "while they were still praying, the place where they were gathered was shaken" (Acts 4:31 CJB). It was when Paul and Silas prayed together that "suddenly there was a great earthquake, so that the foundations of the prison were shaken" (Acts 16:26). Hearing fellow believers pray sharpens the ability to pray biblically, fervently, and comfortably, and expands the vision of what to pray for. Joint praying is invigorating (refreshment and cheer), motivating (incentive, accountability), and energizing (strength and edification). Spurgeon comments, "It is of advantage to others when we use vocal prayer, for it quickens them to the same exercise, as one bird setteth all the rest a chirping....Often one who has been in the spirit of prayer has stirred his friend out of a cold and lifeless frame and set him all on a glow. Yea, and a whole company of believers have been roused to hearty devotion by the fervor of one man."[284]

Joint praying possesses promise and power. When two or more believers pray in agreement, make requests based on the will of God and that which is appropriate in Jesus' name, "it shall be done for them" (Matthew 18:19). Gurnall says, "There is a wonderful prevalence in the joint prayers of His people. When Peter was in prison, the Church meets and prays him out of his enemies' hands. A prince will grant a petition subscribed by the hands of a whole city, which maybe he would not at the request of a private subject, and yet love him well, too. There is an especial promise to public prayer: 'Where two or three.'"[285] R. A. Torrey writes, *There is power in united prayer*. Of course, there is power in the prayer of an individual, but there is vastly increased power in united prayer. God delights in the unity of His people and seeks to emphasize it in every way, and so He pronounces a special blessing upon united prayer."[286]

Chapter 34

Public Praying

"Public prayer will never make up for closet communion."[287] ~ George Müller

Two men in a field spotted an angry bull. As they fled to the nearest fence, it became obvious they wouldn't outrun it, so the one shouted to the other to pray. The companion answered, "I can't. I've never made a public prayer in my life." The friend replied, "You have to! The bull is closing in on us." Finally, the man agreed to pray, saying, "I'll say the only prayer I know, the one my father used to repeat at the table: 'O Lord, for what we are about to receive, make us truly thankful.'"[288] The lesson? The fear of public praying in the church or public arena can be overcome! "To pray in private is essential, but to be able to pray in public is profitable."[289]

Jesus didn't tell believers to refrain from public prayer, just not to engage in it with the ostentation of the Pharisees (Matthew 6:6). He engaged in public prayer and authorized its practice by others.

Pointers to efficacious public prayer.

Public prayers ought not to be mini-sermons. Public prayers ought not to be lengthy. Long public prayers irritated the evangelist D. L. Moody. On one occasion he told Ira Sankey, the song leader, "Lead us in a hymn while our brother is finishing his prayer."[290] That same evangelist said, "A man who prays much in private will make short prayers in public."[291] As Andrew Murray states, it's better for people to wish the prayer were longer than spend valuable time wishing it was over.[292]

Public prayers ought not to be filled with repetitious phases such as, "And Lord! And Lord! And Lord!"[293] (In talking with friends, frequent use of their names is not necessary; neither is it with God.) Spurgeon says, "When 'Dear Lord' and 'Blessed Lord' and 'Sweet Lord' come over and over again as vain repetitions, they are among the worst of blots."[294]

Let the public prayer spring from the private prayer. To only pray in public, or more in public than in private, reveals a pharisaic motive. If you don't pray privately, don't pray publicly, for that would be hypocrisy.[295] Saith Spurgeon, "Habitual communion with God must be maintained, or our public prayers will be vapid or formal."[296]

Keep public prayer appropriate for those assembled.[297] Keep public prayer vibrant, energetic, not sleepy and hollow. Keep it aimed at the heart of God, not the ear of man. And finally, prepare the *heart* for public prayer, not the prayer *per se*.[298] What errand would the Holy Spirit have you take to the Lord on behalf of those gathered? What promises ought to bolster the errand or petition? What needs exist among the assembled? To so ponder, Spurgeon says, "is surely better than coming to God at random, rushing before the throne at haphazard without a definite errand or desire."[299] In Spurgeon's *Lectures to My Students* the pastor will find inspiration and instruction with regard to the pastoral public prayer (something he esteemed so highly that he "would sooner yield up the sermon than the prayer"[300]).

Chapter 35

The Prayer Meeting

"The prayer meeting is the pulse of the church....The prayer meeting is the rallying point where the power of faith in the church concentrates and takes hold on the arm that moves the world....The spirit of prayer and the love and practice of the prayer meeting will so give organic strength to the church as to make her terrible as an army with banners."[301] ~ J. B. Johnston

The cause for few conversions, stalled numerical growth, and stagnation in churches is the desertion of the prayer meeting. James rightly says, "Ye have not, because ye ask not" (James 4:2). More and more churches are relying upon human machinery and organization to accomplish that which God says can be done only supernaturally in response to prayer. "As prayer meetings fail in a congregation," writes J. B. Johnston, "so will the ministrations of the pastor become unfruitful, the preaching of the Word fail to convert sinners and promote holiness in the professors of religion....History confirms the truth that wherever evangelical and vital religion flourish, there lives the earnest gatherings for prayer."[302] Hudson Taylor said, "Since the days of Pentecost, has the whole church ever put aside every other work and waited upon Him for ten days that the Spirit's power might be manifested? We give too much attention to method and machinery and resources, and too little to the source of power."[303] Saith Spurgeon, "The condition of a Church may be very accurately gauged by its prayer meetings. If the spirit of prayer is not with the people, the minister may preach like an angel, but he cannot expect success."[304]

What has killed the prayer meeting? Feeble praying, formalistic praying, faulty praying, faithless praying, fast praying, fruitless praying, fatiguing praying (excessive length in prayer by a brother or sister[305]), and its fusion with a lengthy sermon or Bible study. The best of exegesis will not make a great prayer meeting. J. F. Cowan rightly says, "An ounce of believing prayer is worth a ton of edifying talk. There is great need, in the average prayer meeting, of developing the volume of prayer."[306]

Failure of preparation for and anticipation of the prayer meeting killed it. Saith Moody: "The members should come to the meeting in the spirit of prayer. It ought to be on their hearts from week to week, so they are thinking about it and praying about it."[307]

And all too often the small participation in it has killed it. The value of a prayer meeting is not to be determined by its size. Jesus commended the prayer meeting of just two or more (Matthew 18:19). As W. F. Adeney said, "In listening to prayer, God does not count heads; he weighs hearts. One Elijah stands for more in prayer than a cathedral full of listless worshippers."[308] The bare minimum of saints at a prayer meeting may outweigh in power and effect that of those far larger in attendance. Therefore, never disparage the "two or three" who gather for prayer.

As believers, we must do diligence in reviving the prayer meeting, for it's the oxygen tank that provides life to the church and its various ministries. "Christ meant prayer," saith Andrew Murray, "to be the great power by which His church should do its work, and the neglect of prayer is the reason the church lacks greater power."[309] A challenge from Spurgeon to the believer (and reader): "Go home and say to your minister, 'Sir, we must have more prayer.' Urge the people to more prayer. Have a prayer meeting, even if you have it all to yourself; and if you are asked how many were present, you can say, 'Four.' 'Four! how so?' 'Why, there was myself, and God the Father, God the Son, and God the Holy Ghost; and we have had a rich and real communion together.' We must have an outpouring of real devotion, or else what is to become of many of our churches."[310]

Chapter 36

Prayer and Fasting

"Fasting is calculated to bring a note of urgency and importunity into our praying, and to give force to our pleading in the court of Heaven."[311] ~ Arthur Wallis

Fasting is a Christian's voluntary abstinence from food or any legitimate activity (entertainment, sleep, involvement with people, etc.) for a special spiritual purpose.[312] (Oswald Chambers expands it with regard to the preacher, saying, "Real and effective fasting by a preacher is not fasting from food, but fasting from eloquence, from impressive diction, and from everything else that might hinder the Gospel of God being presented."[313]) Fasting combined with prayer and the proper motive makes it acceptable unto the Lord.

The premise of the fast. The assumption of Jesus was that His followers would fast. He says, "When ye fast..." (Matthew 6:16a).

The privacy of the fast. Fasting is to be done secretively, for the strict audience of God alone (Matthew 6:16–18). The principle cited about giving to the poor is applicable to fasting as well: "Let not thy left hand know what thy right hand doeth" (Matthew 6:3).

The participant of the fast. Fasting is a Christian discipline. It bears no eternal value for the unbeliever because of its God-centered motives and purposes.[314]

The purpose of the fast. William Thrasher states, "The abstinence [fast] is not to be an end in itself but rather for the purpose of being separated to the Lord and to concentrate on godliness."[315] It's not a diet or hunger strike. It's to be practiced for the spiritual reasons set forth in Scripture—to subdue the body's appetites and passions, especially the carnal and evil ones (1 Corinthians 9:27); to prevail with God (Ezra 8:23; Mark 9:29); to liberate from the "yoke" of a sin's mastery (Isaiah 58:6); to give added strength in temptation (Matthew 4:1–11); to provide guidance in making decisions (Nehemiah 1:4); to express mourning and repentance for personal or corporate sin (Joel 2:12–13); to give strength to follow through victoriously with Holy Spirit-led decisions (Esther 4:16); to reveal God's plan for life (Acts 10:10); to drive Satan and the demons of Hell back (Mark 9:17–29); to intercede for a personal enemy (Psalm 35:12–13); to humble the soul (Psalm 69:10; 1 Kings 21:27–29); to break the bondage of physical appetite (1 Corinthians 6:12–13); and to express love and devotion to God (Luke 2:37). Fasting can also turn back the judgment of God upon a nation, as was the case with Nineveh (Jonah 3:5, 10).

The precaution of the fast. Guard against the fast as being a display of religious piety, the means of self-glorification and commendation, and a selfish effort to manipulate the hand of God. Further, Matthew Henry cautions, "If the solemnities of our fasting, though frequent, long, and severe, do not serve to put an edge upon devout affections, to quicken prayer, to increase godly sorrow, and to alter the temper of our minds and the course of our lives for the better, they do not at all answer the intention, and God will not accept them as performed to Him."[316]

The period of the fast. Scripture cites no set or required timetable to fast. Christians are free to fast when and for whatever duration desired.

The power of the fast. To the disciples who were unable to cast out the demon in a boy, Jesus said, "This kind can come forth by nothing, but by prayer and fasting" (Mark 9:29). There are some things that cannot be done apart from prayer and fasting. What can fasting do? Bill Bright states, "Through fasting and prayer, the Holy Spirit can transform your life. When God's people fast with a proper biblical motive—seeking God's face, not His hand—with a broken, repentant, and contrite spirit, God will hear from Heaven and heal our lives, our churches, our communities, our nation, and our world. Fasting and prayer can bring about revival—a change in the direction of our nation and the nations of earth, and the fulfillment of the Great Commission."[317]

The promise of the fast. "And thy Father, which seeth in secret, shall reward thee openly" (Matthew 6:18). "Despite all secrecy, everything remains visible to God (Psalm 33:13–15), and He repays according to what He sees (Proverbs 24:12; Ecclesiastes 12:14)."[318] God promises to do through prayer and fasting things that otherwise will not be possible (Mark 9:29). The full extent of the "reward" (its nature and bestowal) is not indicated.

The prerogative of the fast. Fasting is not to be practiced as a legalistic duty or church obligation. It is to be a voluntary discipline engaged in based upon proper motivation and purpose (Isaiah 58:6). Don't turn that which God ordained to be a willing delight into a legalistic chore.

The practice of the fast. A fast may be without food or water, no food, or some food. Its duration may be one meal or a day or days. If one is medically able to fast, the question for the believer is not should I fast, but when should I fast, how long should I fast, and for what purpose? Let us remember the words of Jesus as we ponder the fast: "This kind can come forth by nothing, but by prayer and fasting."

Chapter 37

Warfare Praying

"Most of our prayers are just asking God to bless the work and to bless some folks that are ill and to keep us plugging along, to keep the work going. But prayer is not merely prattle; it is warfare. Real prayer engages in battle."[319] ~ Alan Redpath

Spiritual warfare may be compared to actual combat, the objective of which is the control of a people or territory or political power. Spiritual warfare is the battle for the control of man's soul and destiny and that of kingdoms of the earth. And its war room is the inner chamber of prayer, the Storm Center on the Battlefield (as Andrew Murray called it) where the believer, shut up with God, participates with Him in battling darkness (Ephesians 6:12). It is there that believers solicit God to beat back the forces of evil, loosen the Devil's grip upon the church and souls, frustrate satanic plans, take back that which belongs to Him and His people, and advance the cause of righteousness (2 Corinthians 10:4–5). Therefore, as Gordon Watt says, "Prayer is not merely a closet exercise of personal communion, but an acting with God in His battle against evil."[320] It's warfare praying. "The power of prayer," writes Bounds, "is most forceful on the battlefield in the midst of the noise and strife of the conflict."[321]

1. Warfare praying is targeted at Satan and his legions of workers. Satan is for real and is working on planet earth savagely, deceitfully, and hideously. He hates the believer and the cause of Christ "with cruel hatred" (Psalm 25:19) so intensely that he "as a roaring lion, walketh about, seeking whom he may devour" (1 Peter 5:8). It is to Satan and the demons to which Paul refers in saying that "we wrestle not against flesh and blood, but against principalities, against powers, against the rulers of the darkness of this world, against spiritual wickedness in high places" (Ephesians 6:12). Satan's activity is increasingly overt and aggressive because he knows that soon the church will be raptured to Glory. "But woe to you, earth and sea, because the devil has come down to you. He is filled with rage, for he knows that his time is short" (Revelation 12:12b NCB). Satan is a mighty foe but not an invincible or invulnerable one, with God in the equation. John reminds us, "Greater is he that is in you, than he that is in the world" (1 John 4:4).

2. Warfare praying is praying with kingdom authority. Christ authorizes saints to storm the counsel room of the Almighty in His name with bold petitions that are founded upon His will and Word. In John 14, He says to them, "If you ask anything in My name, I will do it" (v. 14 NKJV). See Luke 10:19. J. C. Ryle states, "The name of Jesus is a never failing passport for our prayers. In that name, a person may draw near to God with boldness and ask with confidence. God has engaged to hear him."[322] In Jesus' name (kingdom authority) saints possess the power "over all the power of the enemy" (Luke 10:19). Saith Matthew Henry, "You shall tread upon all the power of the enemy, and the kingdom of the Messiah shall be everywhere set up upon the ruins of the Devil's king-dom."[323] See Psalm 91:13. Warfare praying "is repeating the victor's name (Jesus) into the ears of Satan and insisting on his

retreat."[324] Watt says, "If we can but catch the full vision of Calvary as God's pledge of complete victory over the powers of darkness...we shall find timidity in prayer giving place to courageous faith, and the conviction deepening in the spirit that, in alliance with the Holy Ghost, we can by the authority of Him who is enthroned in glory through the Cross remove mountains, pull down strongholds, deliver captives from prison houses, and see the victory won."[325]

3. Warfare praying originates in Heaven. It takes its cues as to what to pray and when from the Holy Spirit. Adrian Rogers says, "Prayer is the Holy Spirit finding a desire in the heart of the Father, putting that desire in our heart, then sending it back to Heaven in the power of the cross. The prayer that gets to Heaven is the prayer that starts in Heaven. Our part is just to close the circuit."[326]

4. Warfare praying is faith based. Its foundation, impetus and confidence are trust that God engages the enemy in response to the prayers of the saint. E. M. Bounds says, "Everywhere in His Word God conditions His actions on prayer. Everywhere in His Word His actions and attitude are shaped by prayer. Prayer puts God's work in His hands and keeps it there. It looks to Him constantly and depends on Him implicitly to further His own cause. Prayer is but faith resting in, acting with, and leaning on and obeying God."[327]

5. Warfare praying includes intercession for fellow soldiers. It beckons God to supply power and provision to Christian soldiers fighting the same battle in the uttermost parts of the earth. It is to pray: "If thy people go out to battle against their enemy, whithersoever thou shalt send them, and shall pray...Then hear thou in heaven their prayer and their supplication, and maintain their cause" (1 Kings 8:44–45). Watt says, "To be in partnership with the risen, interceding Christ is the great call of the Cross to each believer, for whatever else we may not be fitted to accomplish, we can pray. God's supreme need in His Church can be answered by the

weakest Christian."[328] Derek Prime said, "Christians who neglect corporate prayer are like soldiers who leave their front-line comrades in the lurch."[329]

6. Warfare praying precedes battlefield fighting. Battles with the archenemy of the soul and righteousness are not won in the pulpit or church, or by protest. They are fought and won in the prayer closet. To battle Satan with the arm of the flesh, ingenuity, and weaponry is futile. Victorious warriors are they who say, "For I will not trust in my bow," for my sword cannot save me (Psalm 44:6); and, "With him [man] is an arm of flesh; but with us is the LORD our God to help us, and to fight our battles" (2 Chronicles 32:8); and boast with the psalmist, "Praise be to the LORD my Rock, who trains my hands for war, my fingers for battle" (Psalm 144:1 NIV).

7. Warfare praying is prayer that beats back the powers of darkness. Watt says, "Do not pray only for the blessing of God in Christian work, but with equal might and faith pray against the blight of the kingdom of evil. Pray out lies; pray in truth. Pray out the forces of deception and destruction; pray in the life and light of the Lord."[330] Sam Storms states, "To pray effectively against Satan's activity, we must be cognizant of the many ways he seeks to destroy our faith."[331]

8. Warfare praying is to be constantly engaged in. David Brainerd said, "I have ever found that when I have thought the battle was over and the conquest gained, and so let down my watch, the enemy has risen up and done me the greatest injury."[332] And as Spurgeon comments, "The trumpet still plays the notes of war. You cannot sit down and put the victory wreath on your head. You do not have a crown. You still must wear the helmet and carry the sword. You must watch, pray, and fight. Expect your last battle to be the most difficult, for the enemy's fiercest charge is reserved for the end of the day."[333] Maintain agonizing prayer against the enemy in season and out, and in every circumstance of life.

Sleep not, soldier of the cross;
   Foes are lurking all around.
Look not here to find repose;
   This is but thy battleground.

~ Elizabeth C. Gaskell (1848)

The believer can participate with God in battling Satan through warfare praying from any spot on earth (hospital, nursing home, ministry post, home, sickbed, church, prison, battlefield). Let's engage in war on the floor against the satanic forces of darkness that are desecrating and demolishing all that is holy, pure, and godly. Let us pray for fellow soldiers to be emboldened and empowered by the Holy Spirit to stand steadfastly against the evil one, and war a good warfare against him and the armies of Hell. Pray for God's rule to once again reign supremely throughout the land. Unless the church and the saints engage in warfare praying, we stand no hope of overcoming the swelling tide of evil.

Chapter 38

Spontaneous/Ejaculatory Prayer

"*I consider ejaculatory prayer to be the very best form of prayer.*"[334] ~ C. H. Spurgeon

"Most of our praying," says John MacArthur, "should be the extempore outpouring of hearts that are always seeking God."[335] Oswald Chambers states, "Inarticulate prayer, the impulsive prayer that looks so futile, is the thing God always heeds. The habit of ejaculatory prayer ought to be the persistent habit of each one of us."[336]

Ejaculatory or spontaneous prayer is exemplified by Peter when drowning, saying, "Lord, save me" (Matthew 14:30). It is exemplified by Nehemiah's pausing to pray before responding to King Artaxerxes (Nehemiah 2:4). Ejaculatory prayer "as it were, hurls a dart and then it is done."[337] It is prayer that ascends suddenly and briefly to God (a few words or choice few sentences). It is prayer that is sandwiched between a need and its confrontation. Spurgeon said, "And I recommend this [ejaculatory prayer], because it hinders no engagement and occupies no time. You may breathe a prayer to Heaven and say, 'Lord, keep me.' It will take no time. It requires you to go to no particular place. No altar, no church, no so-called sacred place is needed; but wherever you are, just such a little prayer as that will reach the ear of God and win a blessing. Such a prayer as that can be offered anywhere, under any circumstances."[338]

PART FOUR
Practice of Prayer

Chapter 39

The Peril of Prayerlessness

"To be guilty of the sin of prayerlessness is to be guilty of the worst form of practical atheism. It is actually saying we can get along without His help, while the evidence is very clear on every hand that we cannot."[339] ~ Bruce Willis

God is calling us to extraordinary prayer. But for most, sadly, He says, "What! Are you so utterly unable to stay awake and keep watch with Me [in prayer] for one hour?" (Matthew 26:40 AMPC). Bibles are read without prayer; sermons are preached or heard without prayer; decisions are made without prayer; friends are chosen without prayer; dating and marriage partners are selected without prayer; church membership is determined without prayer; possessions are acquired without prayer; money is expended without prayer; houses are built without prayer; and ministry plans are devised without prayer. Saith Samuel Chadwick, "Satan dreads nothing but prayer. His one concern is to keep the saints from praying. He fears nothing from prayerless studies, prayerless work, prayerless religion. He laughs at our toil, he mocks our wisdom, but he trembles when we pray."[340]

Prayerlessness is counted a regrettable spiritual neglect and deficiency. But at its root it's a sin.

It is a sin against God because "it hinders His purposes and prevents Him from accomplishing His mighty works."[341] Some things only come about as the result of prayer (Mark 9:29), and when it is neglected, they go undone. E. M. Bounds said, "If prayer puts God to work on earth, then, by the same token, prayerlessness rules God out of the world's affairs and prevents Him from working. And if prayer moves God to work in this world's affairs, then prayerlessness excludes God from everything concerning men and leaves man on earth the mere creature of circumstances, at the mercy of blind fate, or without help of any kind from God."[342]

Prayerlessness is a sin against the Holy Scriptures, which command us to pray (1 Thessalonians 5:17).

It is a sin against the teaching of Christ who exhorted that the believer should always pray and not faint (Luke 18:1; Matthew 26:41).

It is a sin against the supernatural possibilities that it affords ('We have not, because we ask not,' James 4:2). Andrew Murray wrote, "What is the reason that many thousands of Christian workers in the world have not a greater influence? Nothing but this: the prayerlessness of their service. In the midst of all their zeal in the study and in the work of the Church, of all their faithfulness in preaching and conversation with the people, they lack that ceaseless prayer which has attached to it the sure promise of the Spirit and the power from on high. It is nothing but the sin of prayerlessness which is the cause of the lack of a powerful spiritual life!"[343] Billy Graham said, "A prayerless Christian is a powerless Christian."[344] And Warren Wiersbe says, "Lack of prayer paralyzes us so that we're not able to do anything that will produce lasting fruit to the glory of God."[345]

Prayerlessness is a sin against the soul. Watchman Nee states, "Negligence in prayer withers the inner man."[346] Saith Andrew Murray, "The sin of prayerlessness is a proof that the life of God in the soul is in deadly sickness and weakness."[347] Ole Hallesby has written, "A child of God can grieve Jesus in no worse way than to neglect prayer. Many neglect prayer to such an extent that their spiritual life gradually dies out."[348] John Bunyan said, "Prayer will make a man cease from sin."[349] But neglecting it will make him vulnerable to sin (Matthew 26:41).

Prayerlessness is a sin against the people for whom we are to pray (1 Samuel 12:23). Prayer bears powerful impact upon others; failure to pray blocks that impact.

It is a sin against the mighty power of God available to change world events and stymie the forces of evil.

It is a sin against the work of the church. Spurgeon frankly declared, "A prayerless church member is a hindrance. He is in the body like a rotting bone or a decayed tooth. Before long, since he does not contribute to the benefit of his brethren, he will become a danger and a sorrow to them. Neglect of private prayer is the locust which devours the strength of the church."[350] E. M. Bounds wrote, "What the Church needs today is not more machinery or better, not new organizations or more and novel methods, but men whom the Holy Ghost can use—men of prayer, men mighty in prayer."[351]

It is a sin against society at large. Evil and its instigators could be driven back if saints prayed as they ought to. Jack Taylor said, "Prayerlessness is the source of a host of problems that we battle with today."[352] All identify with D. L. Moody, who said, "Next to the wonder of seeing my Savior will be, I think, the wonder that I made so little use of the power of prayer."[353] Billy Graham states, "We must repent of our prayerlessness. We must make prayer our priority."[354]

"A key rusteth that is seldom turned in the lock." Failure to practice prayer makes it a dread instead of a delight, a chore rather than a choice. "Neglect of prayer makes prayer become hard work, whereas it should be a privilege and a delight. We cannot restrain prayer and yet enjoy prayer."[355] The more frequently the key is turned in the lock of prayer, the greater the pleasure and blessing is prayer.

Early African believers were devoted to prayer, so much so that each had a special prayer spot in the thicket outside the village. Access to these "prayer closets" was made by their feet through the brush. Over time the paths became well worn. In the event grass sprung up on or overtook a trail, it indicated that the believer to whom it belonged had faltered in prayer. Out of concern, when an overgrown "prayer path" was spotted, fellow Christians would say to its owner lovingly, "Friend, there's grass on your path." Grass sown by Satan relentlessly strives to thrive on our prayer path. To prevent its springing up, we must constantly maintain the discipline of prayer, despite the opposition and hindrances presented.

Chapter 40

Plan to Pray

"Without set times of prayer, the spirit of prayer will be dull and feeble. Without the continual prayerfulness, the set times will not avail."[356] ~ Andrew Murray

Believers fail to pray much because they don't plan to pray much. D. A. Carson says, "We do not drift into spiritual life or disciplined prayer. We will not grow in prayer unless we plan to pray."[357] Ole Hallesby said, "If the work of prayer is to be successful, it must also be properly planned. Lack of proper planning will be enough to make the prayer life of many unproductive and ineffective. They have no definite times for prayer, only seasons of prayer as time and occasion permit. Everything is left to the whim of circumstance. And the things they pray for are determined in the same haphazard way, depending in the main upon two things: first, the amount of time they have for prayer and, second, what they at the moment happen to remember to pray for. That will never do. I must know what work I have to do in my secret prayer chamber before I enter into it, what persons and what branches of the work of the kingdom of God I am to take to God in prayer."[358]

Fixed prayer times develop the disciplined habit to pray. Saints of old planned to pray at three set times during the day—morning, noon and evening—though not required (Psalm 55:17; Daniel 6:10). David prayed at seven fixed times daily (Psalm 119:164).

E. M. Bounds advises a morning fixed time to pray (if none other). He states, "The closet first, the study and activities second, both study and activities freshened and made efficient by the closet."[359] The missionary Hudson Taylor likewise suggests the day begin in prayer: "Do not have your concert first and then tune your instrument afterwards. Begin the day with the Word of God and prayer, and get first of all into harmony with Him."[360] John Gill wrote, "The morning is a proper time for prayer, both to return thanks for refreshing sleep and rest; for preservation from dangers by fire, by thieves and murderers; and for renewed mercies in the morning; as also to pray to God to keep from evil and dangers the day following; to give daily food, and to succeed in business and the employments of life; and for a continuation of every mercy, temporal and spiritual."[361] Andrew Murray agrees with both Bounds and Gill, saying, "What an inestimable privilege is the institution of daily prayer to begin every morning. Let it be the one thing our hearts are set on, seeking and finding and meeting God."[362]

Starting the day with prayer will enable greater effectiveness and accomplishment in the day's errands, responsibilities and duties. Upon being asked his plans for the next day, Martin Luther replied, "Work, work, from early morning until late at night. In fact, I have so much to do that I shall have to spend the first three hours in prayer."[363]

Interruptions to set times and places of prayer happen. R. W. Dale states, "Our opportunities for prayer are not always the same. Sometimes we must pray alone; sometimes we can pray with others. Sometimes our prayers must be brief; sometimes they may be prolonged."[364] Remain flexible while consistent. See Acts 2:48.

While regular, scheduled times of prayer are advisable, Spurgeon offered a caution. "The habit of regular morning and evening prayer is one which is indispensable to a believer's life, but the prescribing of the length of prayer, and the constrained remembrance of so many persons and subjects, may gender unto bondage, and strangle prayer rather than assist it."[365]

Chapter 41

Always Pray

"I live in the spirit of prayer. I pray as I walk about, when I lie down, and when I rise up. And the answers are always coming."[366] ~ George Müller

Occasional praying won't thwart temptation forever. It won't solve every dilemma. It won't secure permanent peace and consolation. It won't grant sufficient power for ministry. It won't conquer evil and its propagators. It won't sustain through trial. It won't provide every need. It won't hold Satan at bay or take back the ground he took. It won't energize the spiritual life to fever pitch.

Andrew Bonar challenges, "Pray always. Oh, brother, pray! In spite of Satan, pray; spend hours in prayer; rather neglect friends than not pray; rather fast and lose breakfast, dinner, tea, and supper—and sleep too—than not pray."[367] Adrian Rogers said, "The greatest privilege we have is prayer. The greatest failure that most of us have is prayer."[368] The believer is expressly called to maintain the disposition of prayer at all times in four New Testament texts: Ephesians 6:18; 1 Thessalonians 5:17; Luke 18:1, 7.

Ephesians 6:18. "Praying always with all prayer."

"We must always," says Spurgeon, "be in the spirit of prayer. Our heart must be like the magnetic needle, which always has an inclination towards the pole."[369] That same preacher said, "I cannot help praying. Minute by minute, moment by moment, somehow or other, my heart must commune with God. Prayer has become as essential to me as the heaving of my lungs and the beating of my pulse."[370]

What is it to pray always? It is to pray constantly, continually, or at every opportunity (1 Thessalonians 5:17).[371] It is to pray comprehensively, to make everything a matter of prayer. It is to make use of every occasion to engage in ejaculatory prayer.

Albert Barnes states that to always pray means "we are to maintain an uninterrupted and constant spirit of prayer. We are to be in such a frame of mind as to be ready to pray publicly if requested, and when alone."[372] To pray always, says David Jeremiah, means "to be in a constant state of fellowship with God. It means to live in a conscious state of awareness of being in His presence."[373]

1 Thessalonians 5:17. "Pray without ceasing."

It doesn't mean, John MacArthur says, to "pray repetitiously or continuously without a break, but rather pray persistently and regularly."[374] "It is an exhortation," writes P. J. Gloag, "to live in a devotional frame of mind. It is impossible to be always on our bended knees, but we may be in the spirit of prayer when engaged in the duties of our earthly calling. Prayer may be without ceasing in the heart, which is full of the presence of God and evermore communing with him."[375] Saith Billy Graham, "Prayer should not be merely an act, but an attitude of life."[376] "No one should give the answer," says John Chrysostom, "that it is impossible for a man occupied with worldly cares to pray always. You can set up an altar to God in your mind by means of prayer. And so, it is fitting to pray at your trade, on a journey, standing at a counter, or sitting at your handicraft."[377]

Luke 18:1. **"Men ought always to pray, and not to faint."**

Saith Spurgeon, "Our Lord meant by saying men ought always to pray, that they ought to be always in the spirit of prayer, always ready to pray. Like the old knights, always in warfare, not always on their steeds dashing forward with their lances in rest to unhorse an adversary, but always wearing their weapons where they could readily reach them, and always ready to encounter wounds or death for the sake of the cause which they championed. Those grim warriors often slept in their armor; so even when we sleep, we are still to be in the spirit of prayer, so that if perchance we wake in the night we may still be with God."[378]

Luke 18:7. **"And shall not God avenge His own elect [redeemed], which cry day and night unto him."**

Albert Barnes states, "This expresses one striking characteristic of the elect of God: they pray, and pray constantly. No one can have evidence that he is chosen of God who is not a man of prayer."[379] Scripture admonishes the believer to give God no rest in prayer (Isaiah 62:6–7).

All four texts in essence bear the same interpretation, meaning, and application. Warren Wiersbe summarizes them all into one statement: "Make prayer as natural…as regular breathing. Prayer should be the natural habit of our lives, the 'atmosphere' in which we constantly live."[380] E. M. Bounds states, "Prayer should so impregnate the life that every breath becomes a petition, every sign a supplication."[381] And Billy Graham observes, "Prayer shouldn't be casual or sporadic, dictated only by the needs of the moment. Prayer should be as much a part of our lives as breathing."[382]

"A Christian should carry the weapon of all prayer like a drawn sword in his hand. We should never sheathe our supplications. Never may our hearts be like an unlimbered gun, with everything to be done to it before it can thunder on the foe; but it should be like a piece of cannon, loaded and primed, only requiring the fire that it may be discharged. The soul should be not always in the exercise of prayer, but always in the energy of prayer; not always actually praying, but always intentionally praying."[383]

Origen conceived of the whole of the Christian life to be "one connected prayer"—not in the sense of bended knee, clasped hands or bowed body, but in mindset. The thought is that the believer is to weave the thread of prayer throughout the fabric of the day, from rising to retiring, despite busyness and obligation. Fletcher of Madeley, whose whole life was a life of prayer, sought to do just that so much so that he said, "I would not move from my seat without lifting up my heart to God."[384] This avid prayer warrior met people with the greeting, "Do I meet you praying?"[385] Fletcher of Madeley understood what it was to always pray and not to faint. After his example, let's keep the match of prayer always ready to strike.

Chapter 42

Unoffered Prayers

"There cannot be an answer until there is a prayer."[386]
~ Woodrow Kroll

We question unanswered prayers, but what about unoffered prayers? F. B. Meyers said, "The greatest tragedy of life is not unanswered prayer, but unoffered prayer."[387] Matthew Henry says, "Those who expect to receive comforts from God must call upon Him."[388]

A man died, and in Heaven he noticed gigantic warehouses that stretched miles and miles. Curious, he made inquiry. Peter told him they were packaged answers to prayer of all sizes that never were requested. We have not, simply because we ask not, saith James (4:2). "Heaven is full of answers to prayers," states Billy Graham, "for which no one ever bothered to ask."[389] W. A. Criswell said, "The reason we don't have help from Heaven is we don't ask for it. We don't take it to God. We don't make it a matter of prayer. We just rush into it ourselves, make decisions ourselves, plan things for ourselves, and just leave God out of it. Then we wonder why life can be so bleak and so gray, so frustrating and disappointing. We don't have, because we don't ask (James 4:2)."[390]

The promise "Open thy mouth wide, and I will fill it" (Psalm 81:10) belongs to him that prays. There is no promise for the shut-mouthed, for them that refuse to open their windows toward Heaven. Just ask, "open thy mouth wide," thrust open thy windows toward Heaven, and God will do more than requested or thought possible.

Solomon asked for wisdom. God not only made him the wisest of all men but gave him that which was not asked, "riches and honor" (1 Kings 3:13). The prodigal son asked to be treated as a hired servant (Luke 15:19). He was treated as royalty (v. 22). Jacob prayed for food and clothing and safety on his return home to Bethel. Not only did God do as he asked, but profoundly blessed him (Genesis 33:5–11).

Whatever the need or care, ask God. He is able to do above all that we ask or think (Ephesians 3:20). Packages of all sizes of answered prayers await delivery at your asking. And though asking is a simple thing to do, it must be done to receive ("For every one that asketh receiveth," Matthew 7:8). Leonard Ravenhill shares, "The law of prayer is the law of harvest: sow sparingly in prayer, reap sparingly; sow bountifully in prayer, reap bountifully."[391]

Chapter 43

Stay Prayed Up

"If we would not be taken at unawares, we must be watchful in constant actual exercise of faith and uninterrupted personal communion with God."[392] ~ A. F. Muir

Unexpectedly a father brought his demon-possessed son to the disciples for an exorcism. But "they could not" help him (Mark 9:18). Jesus healed the boy, and later inside the house the disciples "asked him [Jesus] privately, why could not we cast him out?" (Mark 9:28). Jesus answered, "This kind can come forth by nothing, but by prayer and fasting" (Mark 9:29). But they didn't have time to fast and pray at that moment. It happened too fast. And that's the point, isn't it? They ought to have been "prayed up" and thus ready to face such an unexpected opportunity of ministry with God's power instead of relying upon their own ability. A life lesson from their experience: maintain a life of prayer and fasting in order to always be ready (endued with the power of the Holy Spirit) for unexpected ministry opportunities and also personal storms.

Chapter 44

Scripture and Prayer

"Prayer and Bible study are inseparably linked. Effective prayer is born out of the prompting of God's Spirit as we read His Word."[393] ~ Billy Graham

One who gives himself/herself to prayer while neglecting the Word is apt to pray unsoundly, ignorantly, ritualistically, and fanatically—therefore, impotently. Warns H. A. Ironside, "Apart from a knowledge of the Word, prayer will lack exceedingly in intelligence; for the objective must never precede the subjective and must not be divorced therefrom."[394]

That is, prayer must always be linked to the Word of God to be authentic. The one stands upon the other. Prayer detached from Scripture truth is void of power or effect. D. L. Moody said, "If we pray without reading the Word, we shall be ignorant of the mind and will of God and become mystical and fanatical, and liable to be blown about by every wind of doctrine."[395]

Ponder the Scripture. The meditation of Holy Scripture feeds prayer. "Keep this Book of the Law always on your lips; meditate on it day and night" (Joshua 1:8 NIV). Saith Dietrich Bonhoeffer, "The more deeply we grow into the Psalms and the more often we pray them as our own, the simpler and richer will our prayer become."[396] John R. Rice said, "If you surrender yourself and do not rush, but meditate on the Word of God, you will find prayer forming in your heart. It is a prayer inspired by the Holy Spirit, a prayer that God will be pleased to hear."[397] The great prayer warrior George Müller, after years of praying apart from meditation on the Word of God, discovered the immense value of incorporating meditation with prayer. He, in his autobiography, states: "My practice had been at least for ten years, as a habitual thing, to give myself to prayer after having dressed in the morning. Now I saw that the most important thing I had to do was to give myself to the reading of the Word of God and to meditate on it, that thus my heart might be comforted, encouraged, warned, reproved, instructed; and that thus, whilst meditating, my heart might be brought into experimental communion with the Lord."[398] Müller's point? Scripture not only feeds or nourishes the soul; it also fuels it for intimate and meaningful communion with God (Psalm 119:50).

Plead the promises of Scripture. E. M. Bounds says, "Promises stored in the heart are to be the fuel from which prayer receives life and warmth."[399] Turn your Bible into prayer. Read, then plead, the promises. Turn them back to God in prayer. Numerous and precious are the promises connected to prayer which we can claim, including Jeremiah 33:3;

Matthew 21:22; John 14:13–14; John 15:7; John 16:23–24; Psalm 10:17; Jeremiah 29:12; 1 John 5:14; Matthew 18:19; and Matthew 7:7–8. Personalize and claim applicable promises, knowing that God is able to bring each to pass. Paul says, "Being fully persuaded that God had power to do what he had promised" (Romans 4:21 NIV). See Hebrews 10:23. Spurgeon said, "The best praying man is the man who is most believingly familiar with the promises of God. After all, prayer is nothing but taking God's promises to Him and saying to Him, 'Do as Thou hast said.' Prayer is the promise utilized. A prayer which is not based on a promise has no true foundation."[400]

Chapter 45

Pray the Armor On

"They who put on the armor of God and use it as they ought are safe and sure, and so may be secure. Those who are without armor can have no hope to stand."[401]

~ William Gouge

The provision of "the armor of God" reveals man's inability and impotency to battle Satan successfully in his own strength. Although God furnishes it, it is our responsibility to intentionally and consistently put it on. The Bible says, imperatively, "Put on [clothe yourself with] the whole armor [panoply] of God" (Ephesians 6:11). Why? To appropriate the strength and power made available (v. 10) so that we "may be able to withstand against the wiles [tactics, schemes] of the devil" employed for our defeat (v. 11). P. T. O'Brien says, "It is only by donning the divine panoply that believers can be properly equipped against the Devil's attacks."[402] Martyn Lloyd-Jones states, "Every single part and portion of this armor is absolutely essential, and the first thing you have to learn is that you are not in a position to pick and choose."[403]

Pray the armor on. Enter into our King's presence and there clothe yourself for warfare with each piece of the armor in prayer. See Ephesians 6:10–17.

Heavenly Father,

I put on the whole armor provided for my victory over Satan.

I put on the Belt of Truth

To the Word of God may I stand faithful and true, despite what happens. May your Word, not my emotions, order my steps this day.

I put on the Breastplate of Righteousness

Help me live righteously and holy by heeding your Word, for it is a mighty shield against Satan's assault.

I put on the Gospel Shoes

Help me be surefooted in battle against Satan and in my salvation by attachment to your Word. May I stand ready to plunge into every opportunity to share the good news of the Gospel.

I put on the Shield of Faith

I choose to trust YOU with whatever happens, because of Your love for me and promises to me. You will repel Satan's fiery darts of doubt and lies that are hurled at me. I will rejoice this day in knowing that nothing can separate me from Your wonderful love and care. Nothing!

I put on the Helmet of Salvation

May my mind be kept from carnal and injurious thoughts by staying fixed upon YOU. Keep my mind under Your constant control.

I pick up the Sword of the Spirit

May I use Scripture to drive Satan back, thwart his work, overcome temptation and win the lost.

I resort to Prayer in the Spirit

May I continuously seek the counsel and strength of the Lord about all things as I walk through this day.

In Jesus' Name I pray, Amen.

Chapter 46

Document Prayer's Efficacy

"Make me sensible of real answers to actual requests as evidence of an interchange between myself on earth and my Savior in Heaven."[404] ~ Thomas Chalmers

"Praying always with all prayer and supplication in the Spirit, and watching thereunto" (Ephesians 6:18). *Watching thereunto.* Stay watchful to see the effect of prayer. A mother sends a letter to her son fighting a war in a strange land and intensely watches for the return of an answer! An author submits a manuscript to a publisher and watches for a reply. A farmer sows seed into the field and watches for it to sprout up from the sod, then into a full stalk of corn ready to be stored in the barn. Even so ought believers, after sending up their prayer, watch for the return of its answer.[405]

Thus Habakkuk 2:1 says, "I will stand upon my watch, and set me upon the tower, and will watch to see what he will say unto me"; and Micah 7:7 says, "Therefore I will look [or look out] unto the LORD; I will wait for the God of my salvation: my God will hear me."[406] In prayer the *looking out* for its answer demonstrates faith, a confidence that God will reply. W. S. Plumer remarked, "Prayer lives in a watchtower. The oratory should be an observatory."[407] Alexander Maclaren wrote, "He will 'keep watch'; that can only mean that he will be on the outlook for the answer to his prayer or, if we may retain the allusion to sacrifice, for the downward flash of the Divine fire which tells his prayer's acceptance. Many a prayer is offered, and no eyes afterward turn to Heaven to watch for the answer, and perhaps some answers sent are like water spilled on the ground for want [lack] of such observance."[408]

Fail not to connect the answer to prayer with its request. It will build your faith. It will prompt praise unto God. It will be cause for rejoicing. The archer that is unconcerned with where his arrow lands is not very astute—nor is he that shoots up a prayer without interest in where it strikes. Record the date and time of a request and the same for its answer. George Müller had documentation for over fifty thousand specific answers to prayers in his journals.[409] Spurgeon said, "If there be anything I know, anything that I am quite assured of beyond all question, it is that praying breath is never spent in vain."[410]

Chapter 47

The Perpetuity of Prayer

"I firmly believe God continues to answer the prayers of His people even after He has taken them to Heaven."[411]

~ Billy Graham

How long is the lifetime of a prayer that is prayed? E. M. Bounds said, "Prayers are deathless. [They] outlive the lives of those who uttered them, outlive a generation, outlive an age, outlive a world."[412] Ole Hallesby says, "The shower of answers to your prayers will continue to your dying hour. Nor will it cease then. When you pass out from beneath the shower, your dear ones will step into it. Every prayer and every sigh which you have uttered for them and their future welfare will, in God's time, descend upon them as a gentle rain of answers to prayer."[413]

Jesus projected part of His highly priestly prayer into the future: "I am not praying for these alone but also for the future believers who will come to me because of the testimony of these. My prayer for all of them is that they will be of one heart and mind, just as you and I are, Father—that just as you are in me and I am in you, so they will be in us, and the world will believe you sent me" (John 17:20–21 TLB). That prayer is being answered in you and me and yet will be in future generations of Christians. Many prayers uttered today, as with Jesus' prayer, will be answered in future generations, long after the believer's exodus to Glory.

Although we may not be alive to meet our children's children and their children's children, etc., our prayers for their salvation, happiness, marriage, and vocation yet will bear great impact upon them. Despite not seeing prayers answered for family and friends to be saved, America brought to her knees in humility and repentance, and ungodly rulers removed from office, pray on. As Wesley Duewel said, "Prayers prayed in the Spirit never die until they accomplish God's intended purpose."[414] Imagine, your prayers today have the power to affect someone one hundred years from now, and longer. Think outside the box when it comes to prayer.

Doubtlessly, you and I, though unaware of it, have experienced or are experiencing answers to prayers uttered in our behalf long ago by family, friends and ministers. Only in eternity will it become clear how those prayers availed to our benefit of godliness, peace, hope, prosperity, and happiness. It's exciting to ponder what answers to prayer we will yet receive.

PART FIVE
Profit of Prayer

Chapter 48

The Power of Prayer

"Prayer is the conduit through which power from Heaven is brought to earth."[415] ~ Ole Hallesby

How powerful is prayer? Saith Bill Bright, "Through prayer alone men and women can be brought to Christ, Christians can be strengthened, holiness infused into their lives, circumstances altered, tragedies averted, perplexing problems solved, governments and kingdoms overturned, forces of evil defeated, and Satan rendered helpless."[416] John Piper said, "Prayer causes things to happen that wouldn't happen if you didn't pray."[417]

How powerful is prayer? Sometimes all it takes is one prayer to change everything. Its power is equal to the bigness of God. Paul declared that God "is able to do exceeding abundantly above all that we ask or think" (Ephesians 3:20). A. W. Tozer said, "Sometimes when we get overwhelmed, we forget how big God is."[418] E. M. Bounds says, "Prayer has to do with God, with His ability to do. The possibility of prayer is the measure of God's ability to do."[419] In this sense prayer can do anything that God can do.

How powerful is prayer? Samuel Chadwick states, "Prayer gives vision in the secret place, intelligence in work, sense in judgment, courage in temptation, tenacity in adversity, and joyous assurance in the will of God."[420]

How powerful is prayer? John Wesley said, "Every new victory which a soul gains is the effect of a new prayer."[421]

How powerful is prayer? Ron Dunn says, "Prayer is like a missile. It can fly at the speed of thought. It can reach any target anywhere, and there is no anti-ballistic missile that can shoot it down."[422]

How powerful is prayer? "The prayer of the feeblest saint who lives in the Spirit and keeps right with God," says Oswald Chambers, "is a terror to Satan. The very powers of darkness are paralyzed by prayer."[423]

How powerful is prayer? Jesus said, "If ye shall ask…I will do" (John 14:14). What prayer asks in faith and in accordance with God's will, Christ will do. How's that for power? James McConkey said, "God, the eternal God of the universe, stands, as it were, like an almighty servant and says, 'If you, my child, will only pray, I will work; if you will only be busy with asking, I will see to the doing.'"[424]

How powerful is prayer? Chrysostom said, "The potency of prayer hath subdued the strength of fire; it has bridled the rage of lions, hushed anarchy to rest, extinguished wars, appeased the elements, expelled demons, burst the chains of death, expanded the gates of Heaven, assuaged diseases, dispelled frauds, rescued cities from destruction, stayed the sun in its course, and arrested the progress of the thunderbolt."[425]

How powerful is prayer? Gordon B. Watt says, "More things have been wrought for God and His Church through prayer than by any other form of Christian service."[426]

How powerful is prayer? Mighty enough to give remedy and resolution to the trials and troubles of life. Saith Melanchthon, "Trouble and perplexity drive me to prayer, and prayer drives away perplexity and trouble."[427]

Power in prayer, Lord, power in prayer!
Here 'mid earth's sin and sorrow and care,
Men lost and dying, souls in despair,
Oh, give me power, power in prayer!
~ Albert Simpson Reitz (1879–1966)

How powerful is prayer? A. T. Pierson says, "Every conspicuous step and stage of progress, directly traceable to prevailing, believing, expectant supplication—every missionary biography, from those of Eliot and Edwards, Brainerd and Carey, down to Livingstone and Burns, Hudson Taylor and John E. Clough—tells the same story: prayer has been the preparation for every new triumph and the secret of all successes; and so, if greater triumphs and successes lie before us, more fervent and faithful praying must be their forerunner and herald."[428]

How powerful is prayer? Spurgeon says, "Prayer...wins answers from God. God does put forth power in answer to prayer."[429]

How powerful is prayer? Potent enough to drive Satan back when we are assaulted. Saith Adrian Rogers, "Say to the Devil, 'Satan in the name of Jesus, through His shed blood, by the power of the Holy Spirit and the Word of God, I come against you. I resist you and every demonic spirit. I command you, get away from me and my family. I command you to leave.'"[430]

In Jesus' name, believers have been given "power...over all the power of the enemy" (Luke 10:19). Satan has to flee when Jesus' name is our plea (James 4:7). And yet, powerful as all this is, J. Hudson Taylor said prayer's "power has never been tried to its full capacity."[431] Obviously, "those who deny the efficacy of prayer, never pray."[432]

Chapter 49

The Possibilities of Prayer

"The possibilities of prayer run parallel with the promises of God."[433] ~ E. M. Bounds

John Henry Jowett remarked, "God's ability to perform is far beyond our prayers—even our greatest prayers! I have asked for a cupful, while He owns the entire oceans! I have asked for one simple ray of light, while He holds the sun! My best asking falls immeasurably short of my Father's ability to give, which is far beyond what we could ever ask."[434]

What does prayer do? It heals the sick (2 Kings 20:1–2), sends forth laborers (Matthew 9:37–38), conquers temptation (Matthew 26:41), defeats and thwarts Satan (Luke 22:31–32), works miracles (Daniel 6:22), changes things (James 5:16–18), comforts and calms (Philippians 4:6–7), provides guidance (Psalm 143:10), saves the lost (Luke 18:13), opens ministry doors (Colossians 4:3), instills wisdom (James 1:5), endues with power for service (2 Thessalonians 3:1), brings revival (2 Chronicles 7:14), grants deliverance (Acts 12:5–11), and gives grace for dying (Psalm 23:4).

Paul states, "Now unto him that is able to do exceeding abundantly above all that we ask or think, according to the power that worketh in us" (Ephesians 3:20). Spurgeon said, "All our perils are as nothing, so long as we have prayer."[435]

More things are wrought by prayer
Than this world dreams of.
~ Alfred Tennyson, *Idylls of the King*

"How vast," states E. M. Bounds, "are the possibilities of prayer! How wide is its reach! It lays its hand on Almighty God and moves him to do what he would not otherwise do if prayer was not offered. It brings things to pass which would never otherwise occur."[436] Spurgeon says, "There are things to be done yet by God which will astonish us beyond measure."[437]

Chapter 50

God's Response to Prayer

"Ignorance of the method in which God answers prayer may cause us to disquiet ourselves with many ungrounded apprehensions."[438] *~ Theological Sketchbook*

John MacArthur said, "If we never gained anything from prayer but the communion with God that prayer really is, that should be sufficient to make prayer a constant thing."[439] But magnificently, in addition to the sweet fellowship with Him that prayer affords, we are assured answers to our requests. Andrew Murray says, "If there is one thing I think the Church needs to learn, it is that God means prayer to have an answer, and that it hath not entered into the heart of man to conceive what God will do for His child who gives himself to believe that his prayer will be heard."[440]

At times we don't know how He will answer prayer, but we know that it will be answered. The answer will be a "yes," a "no," or a "not right now." Whatever the answer to prayer is, it's a win-win situation. "If the Lord does not pay in silver, He will in gold; and if He does not pay in gold, He will in diamonds."[441] Prayer is always answered in accordance with His glory first, then our best good. "God will either give us what we ask," wrote Tim Keller, "or give us what we would have asked if we knew everything He knows."[442]

Don't stop praying! The Lord is nigh.
Don't stop praying! He'll hear your cry.
God has promised, and He is true.
Don't stop praying! He'll answer you.

Don't stop praying! For ev'ry need.
Don't stop praying! The Lord will heed.
No petition to Him is small.
Don't stop praying! He'll give you all.

Don't stop praying! When bow'd with grief.
Don't stop praying! You'll get relief.
Troubles never escape God's sight.
Don't stop praying! He'll make it right.

Don't stop praying! But have more trust.
Don't stop praying! For pray we must.
Faith will banish a mount of care.
Don't stop praying! God answers prayer.

~ Edna Randolph Worrell (1906)

The answer to prayer may be delayed.[443] William Gurnall said, "Some prayers have a longer voyage than others, but then they return with their richer lading at last, so that the praying soul is a gainer by waiting for an answer."[444] The angel of the Lord came to Zacharias, saying, "Zacharias,...thy prayer is heard" (Luke 1:13). It was a prayer from so many years earlier requesting that a child be given, a prayer that he may have forgotten. The answer came, but it was delayed almost a lifetime. Spurgeon wrote, "Be careful not to take delays in prayer for denials; God's long-dated bills will be punctually honored. We must not suffer Satan to shake our confidence in the God of truth by pointing to our unanswered prayers. Unanswered petitions are not unheard. God keeps a file for our prayers—they are not blown away by the wind; they are treasured in the King's archives."[445]

George Müller prayed for the conversion of two men for 62 years. He died without seeing the prayer answered. But at his funeral one of the men was saved; and the other, two years later. Müller's prayer was answered though delayed a long time. God's ways are not as our ways, nor is His time always our time, but we may be assured He will answer—not a moment too soon or too late (Romans 4:19–20). Let's not hurry the Lord in a response to prayer. "Commit your way to the LORD; trust in him and he will do this:...Be still before the LORD and wait patiently for him" (Psalm 37:5, 7 NIV).

The answer to prayer may be unrecognized. God at times answers prayer in a way unanticipated, causing us to fail to see it. It was so with the church that prayed for Peter's release from prison. They prayed fervently and believingly for his miraculous release. They doubtlessly looked for his deliverance in a specific way, and when it came differently, it was met with unbelief (Acts 12:15–16).

The answer to prayer may yet have conditions to be met before it is fulfilled. Some prayer requests bear stipulations (timing, circumstance, faith) to be met prior to their answer. Greg Laurie said, "When we pray and don't see an answer as quickly as we would like, it may be a result of circumstances that we can't see."[446]

The answer to prayer may not be that which was requested. At times we receive exactly what is requested in prayer; at other times, something far better (though we may not think so at the time).

The answer may be found in the silence of God, not in that which is visible and tangible. Oswald Chambers advises, "You say, 'But He has not answered.' He has; He is so near to you that His silence is the answer. His silence is big with terrific meaning that you cannot understand yet, but presently you will."[447] D. L. Moody wrote, "I think we shall find a great many of our prayers that we thought unanswered, answered when we get to Heaven."[448]

The answer to prayer may be the denial of what was asked. Sometimes we know not that for which we ask, and thankfully it's not granted. Matthew Henry writes, "Though God accepts the prayer of faith, yet He does not always give what is asked for. When God does not take away our troubles and temptations, yet if He gives grace enough for us, we have no reason to complain."[449] See 2 Corinthians 12:9.

"God never refuses without reason," wrote Samuel Chadwick. "He knows the past, in which there may be reasons for present disqualification. Forgiven sin may disable. The Lord knows the future as well as the past. The immediate may imperil the future."[450] "So the first thing we ought to do when we hurt is pray, 'Lord, take it away, please.' If He doesn't, ask Him again and continue to ask Him until He tells you that He has a better or a higher plan."[451]

Note, some prayers are not heard by God and therefore go unanswered. The psalmist said, "If I regard [cherish, embrace] iniquity [sin] in my heart, the Lord will not hear me" (Psalm 66:18). And Isaiah declared, "It's your sins that have cut you off from God. Because of your sins, he has turned away and will not listen anymore" (Isaiah 59:2 NLT). See Proverbs 15:29. Unheard and unanswered prayer happens when we willingly harbor sin in our lives.

Matthew Henry says, "If I have favorable thoughts of it [sin]; if I love it, indulge it, and allow myself in it; if I treat it as a friend and bid it welcome, make provision for it and am loth to part with it; if I delight in it after the inward man, God will not hear my prayer, will not accept it, nor be pleased with it; nor can I expect an answer to it."[452] "Nothing hinders prayer like iniquity harbored in the breast and blocks the passage," saith Spurgeon; "if thou listen to the Devil, God will not listen to thee. If thou refuse to hear God's commands, He will surely refuse to hear thy prayers."[453]

> Who would be cleansed from every sin
> > Must to God's holy altar bring
> The whole of life—its joys, its tears,
> Its hopes, its loves, its powers, its years,
> > The will, and every cherished thing! ~ A.T. Allis

To summarize, Spurgeon says, "We are not to expect that God will give us everything we choose to ask for. If we ask for that which is not promised, if we run counter to the spirit which the Lord would have us cultivate, if we ask contrary to His will or to the decrees of His providence, if we ask merely for the gratification of our own ease and without an eye to His glory, we must not expect that we shall receive. Yet, when we ask in faith, nothing doubting, if we receive not the precise thing asked for, we shall receive an equivalent, and more than an equivalent, for it."[454]

Chapter 51
The Proof that Prayer Works

"Thousands and tens of thousands of times have my prayers been answered. When once I am persuaded that a thing is right and for the glory of God, I go on praying for it until the answer comes."[455] ~ George Müller

"The proof that God answers prayer," saith Chadwick, "is in praying."[456] Prayers in Jesus' name based upon Scripture and God's will are accompanied with answers. S. D. Gordon writes, "True prayer never fails. It cannot because it depends on God and on His pledged Word."[457] "It is not a matter of doubt," saith Spurgeon, "as to whether God hears and answers prayer—if there is any fact in the world that is proved by the testimony of honest men, this is that fact!"[458]

Multiplied testimonies attest to diseases cured, monetary needs supplied, marriages restored, lives transformed, accidents averted, jobs provided, protection from harm granted, laborers raised up, doors to ministry opened, great works done, and revival fires ignited through the efficacy of prayer. Various authors define what constitutes a Bible prayer in different ways, of course, but according to one source, Scripture itself cites answers to approximately 450 prayers.[459] Indisputable proof of the efficacy of prayer is manifest in every Christian's conversion. Upon praying for forgiveness and mercy to be saved, their life was instantly and miraculously transformed (Psalm 34:6).

Proof of Answered Prayer

Jehoshaphat, king of Judah, received a frightening report: "A vast army is coming against you!" Alarmed, Jehoshaphat stopped what he was doing and prayed: "O our God, will You not judge them? For we have no power against this great multitude that is coming against us; nor do we know what to do, but our eyes are upon You" (2 Chronicles 20:12 NKJV). Jehoshaphat and the people prayed for divine help. "All Judah, with their little ones, their wives, and their children, stood before the LORD" (2 Chronicles 20:13). God responded favorably to their prayer and gave them the victory in the battle. Hannah prayed that God would give her a son (1 Samuel 1:1–20). And He did, with the birth of Samuel. Peter in prison awaiting execution was prayed for by the church. As they prayed, an angel of the Lord came to Peter and escorted him to safety (Acts 12:1–17). Elijah prayed for rain, and it rained. He prayed that the rain would stop, and it stopped (James 5:17–18). When God sent the plague of locusts upon Egypt, Pharoah begged Moses to pray for their removal (Exodus 10:17). The record states that God answered Moses' prayer miraculously and removed the locusts until "there remained not one." In travel to Rome by ship, Paul and the crew's lives were in jeopardy amidst a great storm. Paul took a long absence from others to pray, and all aboard were saved (Acts 27:21).

All through the sacred pages of God's Word, miracle after miracle is recorded in response to the prayer of faith. E. M. Bounds says, "Miracles and faith went hand in hand. They were companions. The one was the cause; the other was the effect. The miracle was the proof that God heard and answered prayer."[460] Miracles, happenings that defy human comprehension or explanation and transcend the laws of nature, yet happen today when God's people dare exhibit faith in their asking as those of olden days did. The proof of the power of prayer is in its answer.

The Welsh Revival of 1904

The Welsh revival, suddenly, *in response to prayer*, sprang up and swept across the nation. People crowded into the three daily services (10 a.m.–12 midnight) in the churches. "Saints were revived; infidels were saved; hundreds of drunks, thieves and thugs were born again; and multitudes of the most prominent and socially respected were converted. Additionally, debts were settled, theaters and pubs went out of business, and the mules in the mines couldn't work due to the new vocabulary of the converted workers."[461] Let us pray, "Do it again, Lord; do it again, but here in America."

Moody and the sickly, shut-in prayer warrior

D. L. Moody experienced grave difficulty preaching at a church in London in its morning service. The audience was respectful but not responsive. With reservation he stood to preach to the church that night. And again, he was met with difficulty. However, about half-way through the sermon, the windows of Heaven opened, and the glory of God poured out. Scores of people were saved. The meeting continued for ten days, resulting in over 400 conversions. Moody wanted to know what turned a cold and lifeless service into a Heaven-sent revival. Soon he learned it was the prayers of a bed-ridden elderly saint prayer-warrior that had prayed two years for him to come to the church (unknown to others) and who fasted and prayed for that specific service.

> He answered prayer, so sweetly that I stand
> Amid the blessing of His wondrous hand
> And marvel at the miracle I see,
> The favors that His love hath wrought for me.
> Pray on for the impossible, and dare
> Upon thy banner this brave motto bear,
> "My Father answers prayer." ~ Author Unknown

Müller and 2,000 orphans fed

The famous pastor A. T. Pierson was an overnight guest at the orphanage of George Müller in London. Unknown to Pierson, as it was to all others except Müller, was the absence of food to feed the children the following morning at breakfast. With the 2,000 children in bed, Müller shared the need with him as they met for prayer. They prayed, then slept and awakened to a bountiful breakfast for the orphans at the usual time. Neither man ever learned how the answer to their prayer came. But history informs us. Simon Short of Bristol, unaware of the need, was awakened by the Lord in the middle of the very night that the two men prayed to send food to Müller's orphanage.[462]

The Hundred-Year Prayer Meeting

Some Moravians in the spring of 1727 began praying for revival. By late summer almost fifty of them had committed to praying for one hour a day one after the other, for 24 consecutive hours, seven days a week. The Moravians maintained this round-the-clock prayer vigil for over a century ("The Hundred-Year Prayer Meeting").[463] The prayer ministry resulted in revival and a global missionary awakening among the Moravians. Nathan Finn said, "The Moravians became the tip of the spear for evangelical global missions."[464]

Spurgeon's personal experience

C. H. Spurgeon testified to the proof of prayer's efficacy: "I am constantly witnessing the most unmistakable instances of answers to prayer. My whole life is made up of them. To me they are so familiar as to cease to excite my surprise, but to many they would seem marvelous, no doubt. Why, I could no more doubt the efficacy of prayer than I could disbelieve in the law of gravitation. The one is as much a fact as the other, constantly verified every day of my life."[465]

In 1866 at a Monday evening prayer meeting at the Metropolitan Tabernacle, Spurgeon told his people, "Dear friends, we are a huge church and should be doing more for the Lord in this great city. I want us tonight to ask Him to send us some new work. And if we need money to carry it on, let us pray that the means also be sent."[466]

Unknown to Spurgeon, God immediately began to work in answer to that prayer. A widow, Anne Hillyard, had read Spurgeon's article in *The Sword and Trowel* entitled "The Holy War of the Present Hour," which cited the need for greater ministry to children, and it prompted her to invest in a work dear to her heart—fatherless boys. Not knowing how to proceed, she asked a friend for the name of a reliable person to undertake such an enterprise, and the name of Spurgeon was immediately given.[467]

A few days afterward, Spurgeon received a letter from the widow stating she wanted to contribute the sum of 20,000 pounds ($100,000 at that time) for an orphanage to train and educate orphan boys and asked for his assistance. At her request, William Higgs and Spurgeon paid a visit to her home to discuss the matter. Spurgeon suggested she give the money to George Müller's orphanage, but she was insistent that he use the money in London to establish the work.

As Spurgeon and Higgs left her home, they remarked one to the other how God was evidently answering the prayer uttered a few nights earlier. Within a month, two and a half acres of land were purchased close to the church, and in time the facility was erected that housed 250 boys and 250 girls.[468] And it happened as a result of one prayer uttered at a Monday evening church prayer meeting.

In S. B. Shaw's book *Touching Incidents and Remarkable Answers to Prayer,* readers find numerous documented accounts of answered prayers from the experience of trusted saints like C. H. Spurgeon, D. L. Moody, Charles Finney, John Wesley, T. DeWitt Talmage, and George Müller that will spur faith in the power of prayer.

Chapter 52

Nehemiah: Benefits in Prayer

"Prayer is the ship which bringeth home the richest freight—the soil which yields the most abundant harvest."[469] ~ C. H. Spurgeon

Nehemiah benefited mightily from constant prayer. Prayer revealed the call to him to rebuild the walls about Jerusalem and restore worship in the Temple (Nehemiah 1:4–11). It granted him permission to talk to the king and gain his favor with the project through authorizing it and supplying the material to undertake it. It gave him the strategy and "Holy Spirit engineering" required for the work. (He didn't have a *How to Fix a Wall* handbook. Prayer revealed each step to take in building it.) It fortified him from the harm of railing accusations and assaults of the enemy. It afforded him support in the project from almost all the people in the city. It bolstered his courage not to back down to the enemy's threats and tricks—or quit the work out of cowardice. It provided discernment when he was ill advised to hide, when told of an assassination plot on his life. It gave him a refuge from the slander and lies propagated about him. It kept him focused on the task, unworried by the hostile opposition.

Alan Redpath says, "Did Nehemiah panic or get very worried? Did he answer back or retaliate? Not a bit of it. He just kept on building and ignored them."[470] He steadfastly trusted the Lord and therefore resorted to and relied upon prayer continuously (fourteen recorded prayers in the short book of Nehemiah) to gain guidance, protection, provision, and power—and through it accomplished in fifty-two days the arduous and onerous task (Nehemiah 6:15). Why was prayer so efficacious and beneficial to him? It was because it, as Alan Redpath says, "was grounded in the Word, founded on the promises, rooted in God's past dealings"[471]—and, I add, engaged in believingly and earnestly.

Nehemiah was an ordinary man such as you and I are, but a man that believed in and depended upon prayer to accomplish a heavenly assignment. Let it likewise be employed to benefit us.

Chapter 53

Prayer Spurs Holiness

"Walking with God down the avenues of prayer, we acquire something of His likeness, and unconsciously we become witnesses to others of His beauty and His grace."[472] ~ E. M. Bounds

Time spent in the presence of God in communion has an undeniable transforming influence and impact for godliness upon a person. R. A. Torrey wrote, "Prayer will promote our personal holiness as nothing else, except the study of the Word of God."[473] Isaiah's upward look to God precipitated the cry, "Woe is me! for I am undone; because I am a man of unclean lips, and I dwell in the midst of a people of unclean lips: for mine eyes have seen the King, the Lord of hosts" (Isaiah 6:5). In God's holy presence, sinful contamination and defilement are revealed, prompting confession, renunciation and repentance, and cleansing (Psalm 51:10).

E. M. Bounds writes, "Prayer has everything to do with molding the soul into the image of God."[474] He continues, "Prayer makes a godly man, and puts within him the mind of Christ, the mind of humility, of self-surrender, of service, of pity, and of prayer."[475] Prayer fans the fruits of the Spirit into full flame. He that spends time with God becomes like God. Joseph Parker comments, "You can tell whether a man has been keeping up his life of prayer. His witness is in his face. There is an invisible sculptor that chisels the face into the upper attitude of the soul."[476]

Saith J. C. Ryle, "What is the reason that some believers are so much brighter and holier than others? I believe the difference, in nineteen cases out of twenty, arises from different habits about private prayer. I believe that those who are not eminently holy pray little, and those who are eminently holy pray much."[477] Additionally, "Prayer is a powerful antidote to, and one of the most effectual safeguards against, worldly-mindedness."[478]

PART SIX
Subjects of Prayer

Chapter 54

Pray for the Persecuted

"Remember them that are in bonds, as bound with them; and them which suffer adversity, as being yourselves also in the body." ~ Hebrews 13:3

That which Paul asked for himself, the persecuted church fervently requests: "Now I beseech you, brethren, for the Lord Jesus Christ's sake, and for the love of the Spirit, that ye strive together with me in your prayers to God for me; That I may be delivered from them that do not believe in Judaea; and that my service which I have for Jerusalem may be accepted of the saints" (Romans 15:30–31).

Practical ways to *pray* for the persecuted:

1) Pray for access to the Bible.

2) Pray for safety from persecutors.

3) Pray for courage like a lion in facing opposition and persecution and prosecution (imprisonment, execution, torture).

4) Pray for secrecy of their hiding places from the hostile.

5) Pray that they may remain in their homeland messaging the Gospel.

6) Pray for Holy Spirit discernment to govern their conduct, conversation, and confrontations; and His empowerment to enable their ministry and perseverance.

7) Pray that the God of all comfort will grant consolation, calm, and encouragement.

8) Pray that the material losses (home, land, possessions, money, stock animals, etc.) incurred for "Christ's sake" will

be restored and/or be provided by their brothers and sisters in the faith around the world.

9) Pray that the cost of litigation (court, lawyer) to secure their vindication and/or freedom from imprisonment be supplied.

10) Pray that God will unite them that are rejected and abandoned by family and friends with other believers.

11) Pray for the ruler and decision makers in their land. Jerry Bridges comments, "Prayer is the most tangible expression of trust in God. If we would trust God for our persecuted brothers and sisters in other countries, we must be diligent in prayer for their rulers. If we would trust God when decisions of government in our own country go against our best interests, we must pray for His working in the hearts of those officials and legislators who make those decisions. The truth that the king's heart is in the hand of the Lord is meant to be a stimulus to prayer, not a stimulus to a fatalistic attitude."[479] See Proverbs 21:1. William Tyndale prayed, "Lord, open the king of England's eyes."[480]

12) Pray that their worship and Bible teaching be unhindered.

13) Pray that God will use their witness to ignite a flame for righteousness, religious liberty, and His cause that neither Satan nor man may extinguish.

Chapter 55

Pray for Laborers

"The number of missionaries on the field is entirely dependent on someone praying out laborers."

~ Andrew Murray

Robert Coleman in *The Master Plan for Evangelism* said, "No, there is no use to pray vaguely for the world. The world is lost and blind in sin. The only hope for the world is for laborers to go to them with the Gospel of salvation."[481] From whence will these laborers [church planters, evangelists, pastors, missionaries, and soul winners] come to work in the harvest? Jesus states they will *come* from prayer. Believers are to pray them "out" into the "field" (Matthew 9:37–38).

E. M. Bounds states, "Missionaries, like ministers, are born of praying people. A praying church begets laborers in the harvest field of the world. The scarcity of missionaries argues a non-praying church."[482] Saith Andrew Murray, "How little Christians really feel and mourn the need of laborers in the fields of the world so white to the harvest. And how little they believe that our labor supply depends on prayer, that prayer will really provide as many as He needs."[483]

The labor shortage of harvest workers that exists is directly linked to the lack of prayer for them to be raised up and thrust out. Ole Hallesby solemnly wrote, "There are people on the foreign mission fields who should never have been there. Some of them have not even been converted to God. And at the same time there are people here at home who should have been missionaries. This is our own fault. We should have prayed about this important matter, prayed that none might be sent out who were not sent of God, and at the same time that those whom God has chosen might not remain at home but really go out into foreign lands."[484]

Arthur W. Pink comments, "It's true that [many] are praying for a worldwide revival. But it would be timelier, and more scriptural, for prayer to be made to the Lord of the harvest that He would raise up and thrust forth laborers who would fearlessly and faithfully preach those truths which are calculated to bring about a revival."[485] "Praying Hyde" is said to have prayed hundreds into the harvest fields of God.

Let's resolve to walk in his steps. Pray specifically for God to thrust laborers into the harvest. Pray for pastors, associate ministers, chaplains, musicians and singers, harvest evangelists, and missionaries to be raised up and utilized in fulfilling the Great Commission. Likewise pray for laymen to be raised up to teach, testify, train, and preach at home and abroad. (Your church will have more laborers if you intentionally pray for them.) See my book *Praying Evangelistically* for more insights into praying out laborers.

Chapter 56

Pray for Revival

"Prayer begets revival, which begets more prayer."[486]

~ Jim Cymbala

"O LORD, revive thy work in the midst of the years" (Habakkuk 3:2). No more timely prayer for the church may be uttered than that by Habakkuk. The church stands in dire need of revival—the return to spiritual vitality and life from sluggishness and decay, by the infusion of fresh wind and holy fire. J. I. Packer says, "Revival is the visitation of God which brings to life Christians who have been sleeping and restores a deep sense of God's near presence and holiness."[487] And the means of revival is prayer. Henry Blackaby said, "All revival begins and continues in the prayer meeting."[488] Habakkuk's prayer for revival serves as a pattern for the church and its members.

Habakkuk's prayer was predicated on need. He prayed for revival because of the deplorable estate of the church and its members. Moral decadence, biblical compromise, prevailing wickedness, and spiritual declension among God's people (such as the case is today) always give cause to pray for revival. Habakkuk voiced prayer for revival while alone. Revival praying always begins in the closet out of view of others. Andrew Murray said, "The coming revival must begin with a great revival of prayer. It is in the closet, with the door shut, that the sound of abundance of rain will first be heard."[489]

But from the closet, revival praying moves to the church. The early church prayed together with one heart and one soul, and three thousand people were saved (Acts 2:41). The disciples had a prayer meeting following their release from prison, and the place was shaken wherein they were gathered, and they spoke the word of God with boldness (Acts 4:31–33). The saints prayed in unison on the day of Pentecost, and a great revival occurred under the preaching of Peter (Acts 1:14). By the request of Esther, the people prayed and fasted, and the Jews were delivered from genocide (Esther 4:16). A. T. Pierson said, "There has never been a spiritual awakening in any country or locality that did not begin in united prayer."[490]

Speaking at a conference in 1917, R. A. Torrey (associate to D. L. Moody) gave this prescription for revival: "Let a few of God's people, they don't need to be many, get thoroughly right with God themselves—the rest will count for nothing unless you start right there; then let them band themselves together to pray for a revival until God opens the heavens and comes down. Then let them put themselves at God's disposal to use them as He sees fit. That will bring a revival to any church, any community."[491] Be persistent to pray for revival in the closet and the church until its flames are ignited.

"Revive thy work." The prophet believed revival was possible at God's hand and through His power. Revival praying is founded upon the belief that God can cause dead bones to live (Ezekiel 37:9–12), that He can breathe new life into dead and languishing churches, carnal and weak saints, and impotent ministries, bringing about spiritual renewal and restoration to kingdom work. Tom Malone emphatically states, "The Bible plainly teaches that a revival can happen anytime or anywhere an individual or a group of people, regardless of how small, meets God's requirements and claims His promises."[492]

Habakkuk's prayer for revival is confined to three short sentences. It's not the length of the prayer that counts, but its strength. "Souls laboring under strong emotion commonly express themselves in brief and broken ejaculations rather than in long and polished periods."[493] Of greatest importance is not how long you pray, but that you pray for revival. Will you set aside time regularly to so pray personally and as a church body?

The prophet didn't pray for the evangelization of the unsaved, but specifically that God would set His people right ("revive" refers to the saved, not the lost). It's good to pray for man's salvation (Romans 10:1), but it's for revival, the awakening among the redeemed of the Lord, specifically and pointedly, that prayer must be voiced the more. The need for revival has never been greater. Pray specifically, "Lord, revive me. Revive the members of the church. Revive the backsliders. Revive the pastor and workers. Revive the prodigal in the far country. Revive the musicians and singers. Revive the compromisers, the cold-hearted, and the complacent. Salvation Army leader Samuel Logan Brengle said, "All great revivals have been preceded and carried out by persevering, prevailing knee-work in the closet."[494]

> Revive Thy work, O Lord;
>> Thy mighty arm make bare.
> Speak with the voice that wakes the dead,
>> And make Thy people hear.

> Revive Thy work, O Lord;
>> Disturb this sleep of death.
> Quicken the smould'ring embers now
>> By Thine almighty breath.

> Revive Thy work, O Lord;
>> Give Pentecostal show'rs.
> The glory shall be all Thine own,
>> The blessing, Lord, be ours. ~ Albert Midlane (1858)

Revival praying is to fervently echo the cry of Habakkuk, "O LORD, revive thy work in the midst of the years." It is to echo the cry of David: "Wilt thou not revive us again: that thy people may rejoice in thee? Shew us thy mercy, O Lord, and grant us thy salvation" (Psalm 85:6–7).

We can't organize revival, but we can agonize at the throne of God in prayer for it. We can't work it up, but we can pray it down. Habakkuk's prayer was founded on faith. Oh, that we had more that prayed like him! Oh, for more to pray like Elijah, by whose faith the windows of Heaven opened!

Andrew Murray writes, "Faith in the promise is the fruit of faith in the Promiser. The prayer of faith is rooted in the life of faith."[495] Oswald Sanders said, "Faith does not require external confirmation, but believes God in spite of appearances."[496] To pray for revival believingly is to look expectantly for its coming.

Pray with the confidence of Spurgeon for revival: "Lord, Thou canst revive us again. We are not so deep in the mire but that Thou canst lift us out. We are not so dead but that Thou canst make us alive. Wilt Thou not revive us again? It is impossible to us, but it is possible to Thee. Lord, one touch of Thy hand, a breath from Thy blessed lips, and it is done. Wilt Thou not revive us again?"[497] Spurgeon concluded, "Brothers, sisters, we believe in God, do we not? And if we do, we believe that whatever state a church is in, God can bring it out of it."[498] And we answer, yes, we do!

Habakkuk acknowledged that revival was God's work and could only occur by His power generating it (Psalm 119:126). Revival gimmickry (fleshly techniques arousing people to walk the church aisle) may imitate revival but never will it duplicate it. Gifted preachers may manipulate hearts to make a "decision," but only God has the power to change hearts.

E. M. Bounds says, "Few Christians have anything but a vague idea of the power of prayer; fewer still have any experience of that power. The Church seems almost wholly unaware of the power God puts into her hand; this spiritual carte blanche on the infinite resources of God's wisdom and power is rarely, if ever, used—never used to the full measure of honoring God."[499]

Saith A. C. Dixon, "When we rely upon organization, we get what organization can do; when we rely upon education, we get what education can do; when we rely upon eloquence, we get what eloquence can do, and so on. Nor am I disposed to undervalue any of these things in their proper place, but when we rely upon prayer, we get what God can do."[500]

The only power that can awaken sleeping saints and dead sinners is that of the Holy Spirit. "The Holy Spirit is the Author of all true quickening of the Divine life in the souls of men, and His renewing and sanctifying influences are secured in response to earnest supplication."[501] Habakkuk may have recalled God's promise about revival in 2 Chronicles 7:14: "If my people, which are called by my name, shall humble themselves, and pray, and seek my face, and turn from their wicked ways; then will I hear from heaven, and will forgive their sin, and will heal their land."

Revival hinges upon the believers' desperation (hunger and thirst), contrition (broken-ness and humility), renunciation (abhorrence and abandonment of sin), confession (repentance and cleansing of sin), supplication (prayer for renewal), and dedication (submission to the Lordship of Christ). When we have met the conditions of revival, it will come—but not before.

Go to God with the prayer of Isaiah: "Oh that thou would-est rend the heavens, that thou wouldest come down, that the mountains might quake at thy presence" (Isaiah 64:1 ASV). Is this not the heart-cry of every saint that recognizes the need of the church and the world? Above the want and need of more laborers, evangelistic-hearted pastors, harvest evangelists, and missionaries, we need the sacred visitation of the presence of the Almighty.

We do not simply want numerical growth and expansion in the church, new strategies to implement, or magnificent sanctuaries; but above all we crave that God will manifest Himself to His people, refresh and revive them, and restore the church to its former glory. Let the church pray incessantly for God to "look down" (Isaiah 63:15) upon its woeful and needy estate with compassion and mercy and then to 'come down' (Isaiah 64:3) into its midst with the quickening, sanctifying, and energizing power of the Holy Spirit.

Chapter 57

Pray for Healing

"This above everything else: when I am sick, let me take myself to God. Let me take myself to God."[502] ~ W. A. Criswell

I agree with Chuck Swindoll when he said, "I believe in divine healing. I do not believe in divine healers. I believe in faith healing. I do not believe in faith healers. There is a great difference."[503] Healing is possible at the hands of God, because the Bible teaches it (James 5:14–16); His name, *Jehovah-rapha* (the healer), declares it (Exodus 15:26); and numerous documented healings in the Bible affirm it.[504] Abraham prayed for Abimelech, and Abimelech was healed (Genesis 20:17). God healed a leprous Miriam (Numbers 12:10–15). God heard Hezekiah's request for healing and added fifteen years to his life (Isaiah 38:1–5). Bartimaeus (Mark 10:46–52) and Jairus' daughter (Matthew 9:18–26) were also healed by Him.

Documentation for divine healing outside the Bible is stated by Alexis Carrel, distinguished physician and philosopher: "As a physician, I have seen men, after all other therapy had failed, lifted out of disease and melancholy by the serene effort of prayer. It is the only power in the world that seems to overcome the so called 'laws of nature'; the occasions on which prayer has done this have been termed 'miracles.'"[505] Spurgeon witnessed such "miracles." It is said that his prayers raised up more sick persons in London than the treatment of any doctor.[506]

James gives instructions to the sick. He writes, "Is any among you afflicted? let him pray....Is any sick among you? let him call for the elders of the church; and let them pray over him, anointing him with oil in the name of the Lord: And the prayer of faith shall save [heal] the sick, and the Lord shall raise him up" (James 5:13–15). To encapsulate, James teaches the incapacitated sick saint to pray for himself (James 5:13), summon the elders (spiritually mature leaders of the church), if desired, to pray, and request the prayers of all the saints (James 5:14). Elders, if summoned, pray in faith specifically for healing and recovery, anointing with oil "in the name of the Lord" (according to God's will and plan). The prayer of faith is primary (the means of healing); the medicinal oil is secondary (evangelicals agree that the anointing with oil bears no "magic" healing power). George Sweeting said, "In my thinking, the 'prayer of faith' cannot be prayed simply at will. It is given of God in certain cases to serve His purpose and to accomplish His sovereign will."[507]

Clearly, it's not God's will to heal everyone. W. A. Criswell comments, "Note that in 2 Corinthians 12:7–10, in which Paul earnestly prays for healing, it does not occur; and in 2 Timothy 4:20, note that Paul's valued friend and helper Trophimus remains sick at Miletus, yet Paul did not heal him."[508] In John 5, we read that although many who were sick surrounded the pool at Bethesda (verse 3), *only* the one man with the infirmity was healed (verses 8–9). Moses pleaded with God, 'O God, let me live; let me go into the land with these people' (Deuteronomy 3:25). And yet he died.

Shadrach, Meshach and Abednego, facing the burning furnace, said, 'Our God is able to deliver us' (Daniel 3:17). They didn't say He *would* deliver them. Whether He did or didn't, they trusted Him to do what was best (verse 18).[509] This is the right attitude and approach to embrace regarding sickness and suffering. Faith says we can always trust the judgment of God to do what is expedient regarding our health. The bottom line of the text seems best put by Max Lucado: "Call out to God for help. Will He do what you want? I cannot say, but this I can say: He will do what is best."[510] See Romans 8:28.

Trust God to do what He counts is best, even though it be not what you want, rather than endeavoring to manipulate Him to do otherwise. Samuel Storms states, "Setting fixed terms which decide whether God performs healing or not nudges us across the border that separates providence from magic and trespasses on God's right to be Lord. It preempts His authority to decide when and how to manifest His power. It makes our conformity to certain conditions rather than His sovereignty the ultimate ground of how He works."[511] The safest prayer and surest foundation in praying for healing, is, "If it be Thy will."

Ole Hallesby suggests we pray: "Lord, if it will be to Your glory, heal suddenly; if it will glorify You more, heal gradually; if it will glorify You even more, may your servant remain sick awhile; and if it will glorify Your name still more, take him to Yourself in Heaven."[512]

Chapter 58

Pray for the Unsaved

"Prayer is crucial in evangelism. Only God can change the heart of someone who is in rebellion against Him. No matter how logical our arguments or how fervent our appeals, our words will accomplish nothing unless God's Spirit prepares the way."[513] ~ Billy Graham

The divine order is to talk to God about man, then to man.[514] "All great soul winners have been men of much and mighty prayer,"[515] said Salvation Army leader Samuel Logan Brengle. John R. Rice wrote, "Our fathers were accustomed to pray, 'Lord, roll on us the weight of immortal souls.' Again and again, I have heard that heartfelt petition as men besought God to give them a Heaven-born concern for the salvation of sinners. That prayer I heard often in my childhood, and I make it my own again today."[516] And may every saint make it theirs also. J. Sidlow Baxter said, "Men may spurn our appeals, reject our message, oppose our arguments, despise our persons, but they are helpless against our prayers."[517]

S. D. Gordon writes, "Man is a free agent, to use the old phrase, so far as God is concerned—utterly, wholly free. The purpose of our praying is not to force or coerce his will—never that. It is to *free* his will of the warping influences that now twist it awry. It is to get the dust out of his eyes so his sight shall be clear. And once he is free, able to see aright, to balance things without prejudice, the whole probability is in favor of his using his will to choose the only right."[518]

David Wilkerson wrestled with praying for the unsaved. He writes, "As a younger Christian, I was often confused by some teaching and preaching that said, in essence, 'God's Word cannot lie. If we ask *anything* in His name, He will do it. God is bound to His Word. He will answer us.' I believed this. However, when it came to praying for unsaved loved ones, I wondered about it in light of the teaching regarding the free will of man. I thought, 'If my prayers can cause a person to turn to Christ, doesn't this trespass man's free will?' I have learned to accept both truths as being possible, yet not contradictory. Through prayer, we can move men toward God. Through prayer, we can see our loved ones come to Christ. I also believe the unsaved have a free will of their own, and they may resist the conviction of the Holy Spirit which comes as a result of our prayers.…We are to pray 'without ceasing' and leave the ultimate outcome in the hands of God and within the decision-making prerogative of the unsaved."[519]

Make a list of names of the lost for which to pray regularly (Romans 10:1). As they are saved, mark through the name, entering the date of their conversion. Frequently add new names to the list. Such praying does not go unnoticed or unanswered. In time God will say, "I have heard thy prayer, I have seen thy tears" (Isaiah 38:5). Specific things for which to pray:

Pray for Cultivation prior to the witness, that the soil in the soul of the sinner may be broken up, seeded, and prepared for the presentation of the Gospel (Hosea 10:12).

Pray for Orchestration of the witness, that the Holy Spirit will lead the right soul winner to this person at the most opportune time to share the Gospel (Matthew 9:38).

Pray for Reception to the witness, that the sinner will be open to the soul winner's presentation.

Pray for Illumination in the witness, that the Holy Spirit will open blinded eyes that divine truth may be revealed and received (Acts 26:18; Acts 16:14).

Pray for Liberation in the witness, that every satanic stronghold in the heart would be destroyed, resulting in total deliverance (Matthew 12:29). Saith Oswald Sanders, "Plead the blood of the Lamb for the liberation of the soul for whom you pray."[520]

Pray for Conviction in the witness, that the sinner will see his disobedience (failure to keep the Ten Commandments) toward God (John 16:8).

Pray for Regeneration in the witness, that the lost person may express godly sorrow regarding his crime against God and in faith receive Jesus Christ as Lord and Savior (Acts 20:21).

Ask of me, and I shall give thee the heathen for thine inheritance (Psalm 2:8). In response to prayer for the unreached there will be a great ingathering from the heathen world. Hallesby writes, "When you begin to grow tired of the quiet, unnoticed work of praying, then remember that He who seeth in secret shall reward you openly. He has heard your prayers, and He knows exactly what you have accomplished by means of them for the salvation of souls. If not before, then on the Great Day, you will come bringing in the sheaves, the fruit of your labors."[521]

In learning he had only thirty minutes to live, a college president said, "Then take me out of bed and put me on my knees and let me spend it calling on God for the salvation of the world." This they did, and he died upon his knees. What a way to meet death!

Chapter 59

Pray for the Minister

"Let me have your prayers, and I can do anything! Let me be without my people's prayers, and I can do nothing."[522]

~ C. H. Spurgeon

Paul's request of the saints at Ephesus is that of every minister: "And [pray] for me, that utterance may be given unto me, that I may open my mouth boldly, to make known the mystery of the gospel" (Ephesians 6:19). Robert M. McCheyne exhorted, "Pray for your pastor. Pray for his body that he may be kept strong and spared for many years. Pray for his soul, that he may be kept humble and holy, a burning and shining light. Pray for his ministry, that it may be abundantly blessed, that he may be anointed to preach good tidings, that there be no secret prayer without naming him before your God."[523]

At its Monday night prayer meeting, Spurgeon pleaded with his congregation for prayer: "As for me, I beg a special interest in your prayers that I may be sustained in this tremendous work to which I am called. A minister must be upheld by his people's prayers, or what can he do? When a diver is on the sea bottom, he depends upon the pumps above, which send him down the air. Pump away, brethren, while I am seeking for my Lord's lost money among the timbers of this old wreck. I feel the fresh air coming in at every stroke of your prayer pump; but if you stop your supplications, I shall perish. When a fireman climbs upon the roof with the hose, he can do nothing if the water is not driven up into it. Here I stand, pointing my hose at the burning mass. Send up the water, brethren! Send up a continual supply! What will be the use of my standing here with an empty hose? Every man to the pump! Let each one do better still; let him turn on the main. The reservoir is in Heaven; every saint is a turncock; use your keys and give me a plentiful supply. What I ask for myself, I seek for every true minister of Christ. Let not one be left to himself. We all cry with one voice, 'BRETHREN, PRAY FOR US.'"[524] Spurgeon again said to his church, "God is my witness how often I have striven in this pulpit to be the means of the conversion of men. I have preached my very heart out. My hearers, I have done my utmost. Will not your prayers accomplish that which my preaching fails to do?"[525]

R. W. Dale likewise pleaded with his congregation for prayer for himself: "You come to listen to me on Sunday, and I have nothing to say that adds vigor to faith or fervor to love, or that enlarges your knowledge of duty or of God. It is plain that during the week I have had no clear vision of spiritual truth, or that, if I have, the vision has faded away. You are naturally disappointed, perhaps discontented. It is partly my fault. But is it not possible that the fault is as much yours as mine? If you had prayed for me with earnestness and faith, might not the vision of God have come to me, and the revelation of spiritual truth and the baptism of fire? In the absence of your intercessions, God may have given me truth for myself, but not for you."[526]

Spurgeon and Dale voice the heart of all pastors regarding the absolute necessity of prayer by their people. Make time to pray earnestly for the man of God as he labors in the study to prepare the message for the Lord's Day, proclaims what God has given, and issues the invitation. "God's servants would preach better," states H. A. Ironside, "if you prayed for them more; there would be more response to the preaching if they were more upheld in the secret closet by the people of God."[527]

E. M. Bounds wrote, "The men in the pew given to praying for the pastor are like poles which hold up the wires along which the electric current runs. They are not the power, neither are they the specific agents in making the Word of the Lord effective. But they hold up the wires upon which the divine power runs to the hearts of men. They make conditions favorable for the preaching of the Gospel."[528] May your pastor say of you (and other believers that make up the church) that which Paul spoke to the Corinthians: "Ye also helping together by prayer for us" (2 Corinthians 1:11).

Chapter 60

Pray for Others (Intercession)

"The man who mobilizes the Christian church to pray will make the greatest contribution to world evangelization in history."[529] ~ Andrew Murray

Petition is praying for ourselves; intercession is praying for others. "Pray one for another" (James 5:16). D. James Kennedy said, "So often we pray narrowly, attending only to our own needs. Instead, we should pray broadly for everyone. We should pray for the lost that they might be saved and for the saved that they might win the lost."[530] "The measure of our love for others," says A. W. Pink, "can largely be determined by the frequency and earnestness of our prayers for them."[531]

God is looking for "gap-men"—intercessors for people, ministries, causes, and nations (Ezekiel 22:30). Intercessors were plenteous in biblical days. Abraham pleaded for Sodom and Gomorrah, Jeremiah for apostate Israel, Samuel for Saul, David for the Jewish people, Daniel for the Israelites in Babylonian captivity, Paul for the saints at Philippi and elsewhere, Epaphras for the Colossian believers; and Christ prayed for Peter and the disciples.

To be an intercessor for another, to bear their sorrows, heartaches, burdens, cares, and needs to the Lord, is the greatest kindness that might be done for them. To have it said of a believer, "He prayed for his friends" (Job 42:10), is most commendable. To pray for self is expected, expedient and good. To pray for others, to become an intercessor, is, however, the greater work.

John Calvin said, "Our prayer must not be self-centered. It must arise not only because we feel our own need as a burden we must lay upon God, but also because we are so bound up in love for our fellow men that we feel their need as acutely as our own."[532] Saith Andrew Murray, "The work of intercession is the greatest work a Christian can do."[533] Samuel Chadwick said, "Who can measure the work of those whose ministry is that of laboring in prayer for others?"[534]

No greater help and care is given
    To others in their need
Than when we bear them up in prayer
    And for them intercede. ~ Dennis J. DeHaan

Chuck Swindoll says, "Be an intercessor. Remember to pray for those in your life who have needs only God can meet."[535] What must be avoided in intercession is ceasing to pray for people before their need is supplied, their spiritual walk is restored, or their brokenness is mended. Every saint has been woefully guilty of abandoning others in intercession. Be steadfast in intercession until the need is supplied or you are released from it by God.

The side benefit of running errands to the King in behalf of others is that we will come away enriched by it. John of Kronstadt said that prayer in behalf of another benefits the man who prays in three ways: "It purifies the heart, strengthens faith and hope in God, and arouses love for God and our neighbor."[536]

Intercessory prayer is limitless and boundless in scope. Richard Halverson says, "No place is closed to intercessory prayer: no continent, no nation, no city, no organization, no office. No power on earth can keep intercession out."[537] Wesley Duwel comments, "Not only can prayer reach Heaven, but the arm of prayer can span the miles to any part of the world; and you in your place of intercession can touch someone who needs you, even thousands of miles away. This is not make-believe. It is spiritual reality."[538] T. J. Bach says, "Many of us cannot reach the mission fields on our feet, but we can reach them on our knees."[539]

As the practice of intercession helps, so the neglect of it hurts others, God's cause, and ourselves. Failing to engage in it is a sin against the Lord (1 Samuel 12:23). The one thing that is said to have surprised God is that the voice of intercession had ceased: "And he saw that there was no man, and wondered that there was no intercessor" (Isaiah 59:16). His delivering mercy depends upon intercessors who will put their shoulders under the burdens of others: "And I sought for a man among them, that should make up the hedge, and stand in the gap before me for the land, that I should not destroy it: but I found none" (Ezekiel 22:30).

Charles Finney was at times preceded to revivals by a man named Daniel Nash who prepared the way in prayer for his ministry. On one occasion a woman approached Finney and said,

"About a week ago, Mr. Nash rented a room from me. After three days, I wondered why he hadn't come out of his room. I went up to his door and heard him groaning. Thinking something was wrong with him, I opened the door and peeked in. There he was, lying in the middle of the floor, groaning and praying."

"Don't worry about Brother Nash," Finney told her. "He just has the burden of intercession to pray for lost souls." The man was simply praying with groanings that could not be uttered in articulate speech for a mighty movement of God in the city and the salvation of lost souls (Romans 8:26). May more be possessed with the passion of a Nash for lost souls. The normal function of prayer is to be an intercessor as he was.

Chapter 61

Pray for Personal Concerns

"We leave our burdens, worries and sin in the hands of God. We come away with oil of joy and the garment of praise."[540] ~ F. B. Meyers

"Cast thy burden upon the LORD, and he shall sustain thee: he shall never suffer the righteous to be moved" (Psalm 55:22). A poor man with heavy bundles upon his back was offered a ride in a wagon by its wealthy owner. He gladly accepted. After traveling for some distance, the wealthy man noticed that the bundles were yet upon the poor man's shoulders. "Why don't you put your belongings down?" asked the wealthy man. "There is plenty of room in my wagon to lay your burdens down. Are they not heavy?"

"Indeed, they are," sighed the poor man, "but you have been more than gracious to offer me a ride, and I do not wish to take advantage of you by weighing down your wagon." Though trying to be considerate, out of ignorance the man acted foolishly. We all too often are like him. We bring our burdens to the Lord in prayer but walk away with them still loaded upon our shoulders.

It is wonderful, surely, to carry your burden
    With a smile and a shrug that seems gay,
While you crush back the heartache and smother your anguish
    If you know of no better way.

But I've found that no trial or heartache or sorrow
    Is too great for my Savior to bear.
So, I take them and give them to His gracious keeping
    And thank Him and leave them there.

And, wonder of wonders, the heart that was breaking,
    The pain that was hurting, the trial
Is no longer my burden, but His, and my portion
    Is gladness, and joy, and a smile.[541]

               ~ Mildred Allen Jefferies

Spurgeon said, "Roll your burden onto the Lord through prayer, and you have rolled it into a great deep out of which it will never by any possibility arise. Cast your trouble where you cast your sins. You have cast your sins into the depths of the sea; *there* cast your troubles also. As soon as the trouble comes, quick, the first thing, tell it to your Father in prayer."[542]

Leave it there; leave it there.
Take your burden to the Lord and leave it there.
If you trust and never doubt, he will surely bring you out.
Take your burden to the Lord and leave it there.

If your body suffers pain and your health you can't regain
    And your soul is almost sinking in despair,
Jesus knows the pain you feel; He can save and He can heal.
    Take your burden to the Lord and leave it there.

               ~ Albert Tindley (1906)

W. S. Plumer says, "If we can bring our woes before God in prayer, we have done the best possible thing."[543]

62

The Minister's Prayer Life

"A minister may fill his pews, his communion roll, the mouths of the public, but what that minister is on his knees in secret before God Almighty, that he is and no more."[544]

~ John Owen

Prayer is the means by which the minister communes with God personally, leads his people corporately, obtains Holy Spirit power and wisdom, and engages in the heavenly task assigned. With it he succeeds; without it, he fails. E. M. Bounds says, "The preacher who is feeble in prayer is feeble in life-giving forces....The man—God's man—is made in the closet. Prayer makes the man; prayer makes the preacher; prayer makes the pastor."[545] James McConkey states, "Words spoken, prayers uttered, acts done in the energy of self alone have no power of spiritual germination. Except the Spirit speak through us, there will be no *quickening* in those about us. The sermon delivered in pride of intellect or rush of mere human eloquence may excite the intellect, arouse admiration, or stir emotion; but it cannot *transmit life*."[546] Without prayer, that which is said, sung or done in the pulpit is but as 'tinkling cymbals and sounding brass' (see John 15:5).

Alistair Begg writes, "There is no chance of fire in the pews if there is an iceberg in the pulpit; and without personal prayer and communion with God during the preparation stages, the pulpit will be cold."[547] Thomas Armitage states, "A sermon steeped in prayer on the study floor, like Gideon's fleece saturated with dew, will not lose its moisture between that and the pulpit. The first step towards doing anything in the pulpit as a thorough workman must be to kiss the feet of the Crucified, as a worshipper, in the study."[548] Therefore the advice of McCheyne is worthy of heed: "Give yourself to prayer, and get your texts, your thoughts, your words from God."[549] And then beg God, as Elijah did on Mt. Carmel, to send the fire of the Holy Spirit to empower the delivery and the reception, to the end that lives are miraculously changed. Says Spurgeon, "Prayer will singularly assist you in the delivery of your sermon; in fact, nothing can so gloriously fit you to preach as descending fresh from the mount of communion with God to speak with men. None are so able to plead with men as those who have been wrestling with God on their behalf."[550] Saith Harry Ironside, "If we would prevail with men in public, we must prevail with God in secret."[551]

He that develops and delivers the sermon in prayer may say with Criswell, "I wasn't wrapped in my own academic robes on the Lord's Day. I wasn't hiding behind all the degrees I have tried to win on the Lord's Day. I wasn't trying to say what man would say on the Lord's Day. I was in the Spirit on the Lord's Day. When I walked into the pulpit, it might have been "pore" English, faulty construction, and homiletically unsound; but when I stood there, such as I was and what I could do, that did I say and preach in the power of the Holy Spirit."[552] Amen and amen.

63

The Judge's Prayer

"All magistrates act in His name, and by virtue of His commission. He is invisibly present at their assemblies and superintends their proceedings. He receives appeals from their wrongful decisions; He will one day rehear all causes at His own tribunal and reverse every iniquitous sentence before the great congregation of men and angels."[553] ~ George Horne

Upon Abraham Lincoln's securing the Republican Party's presidential nomination, Joshua Giddings sent a letter of congratulations in which he urged him to "avoid corrupting influences." Lincoln, on May 21,1860, responded, saying, "I am not wanting in the purpose, though I may fail in the strength, to maintain my freedom from bad influences. Your letter comes to my aid in this point most opportunely." Lincoln then closed the letter with words that form a prayer for all judges. "May the Almighty grant that the cause of truth, justice, and humanity shall in no wise suffer at my hands."[554] *The Judge's Prayer* ought to be emblazoned upon the heart of every judge and inscribed upon the wall of their offices.

Extend gratitude to judges and magistrates for serving our Lord honorably and rightly. Pray they will not become tainted by corrupting influences and will always have courage to do what is right, regardless of political pressure or personal cost.

64

Life's Final Prayer

"May we spend our days, and end our lives, praying for the spread of His Gospel."[555] ~ Matthew Henry

David, under the inspiration of the Holy Spirit, foresaw the rule and redemptive act of the Messiah, the Lord Jesus Christ, through the prophetic front window of the future (Psalm 72). We view it through the back window of established history, seeing it wondrously fulfilled and saying with David, "Blessed be his glorious name forever: and let the whole earth be filled with his glory; Amen, and Amen" (Psalm 72:19). Matthew Henrys says, "How he ever shuts up his life with this prayer (v. 20). This was the last Psalm that ever he penned, though not placed last in this collection; he penned it when he lay on his deathbed, and with this he breathes his last: 'Let God be glorified; let the kingdom of the Messiah be set up, and kept up, in the world, and I have enough; I desire no more. With this let the prayers of David the son of Jesse be ended. Even so, come, Lord Jesus; come quickly.'"[556] There is no more pertinent prayer to pray presently and, most certainly, as the last prior to our exodus to Heaven.

"We too will cease from all petitioning if it be granted to us to see the day of the Lord. Our blissful spirits will then have nothing further to do but for ever to praise the Lord our God."[557] Amen, and amen.

Sweet hour of prayer! Sweet hour of prayer!
May I thy consolation share,
Till, from Mount Pisgah's lofty height,
I view my home and take my flight.

This robe of flesh I'll drop, and rise
To seize the everlasting prize,
And shout, while passing through the air,
"Farewell, farewell, sweet hour of prayer!"
~ William B. Bradbury (1861)

65

To Your Knees!

"Prayer is the acid test of devotion. Nothing in the life of faith is so difficult to maintain."[558] ~ Samuel Chadwick

"Bow down thine ear, O LORD, hear me: for I am poor and needy" (Psalm 86:1). Don't discount the power of prayer. Its force has been manifested and demonstrated over and over again in transforming souls, curing sicknesses, reviving churches, comforting the brokenhearted, resolving problems, restoring relationships, navigating lives, making decisions, and healing nations. W. A. McKay (1890) reminds us, "When Elijah prayed, the nation was reformed; when Hezekiah prayed, [he was] healed; when the disciples prayed, Pentecost appeared; when John Wesley and his companions prayed, England was revived; when John Knox prayed, Scotland was refreshed; when the Sabbath school teachers at Tannybrake prayed, eleven thousand were added to the church in one year; when Luther prayed, the papacy was shaken."[559] With such power available to effect godly change, I enjoin you with the words of McKay: "To your knees, then, ye Christians! Plead until the windows open; plead until the springs unlock; plead until the clouds part; plead until the rains descend; plead until the floods of blessing come."[560] When there is remedy and resolution to the ills of the day in our "closets," let us often avail ourselves of it, personally and corporately. As the Scripture says, "Ye have not, because ye ask not" (James 4:2).

> Thou art coming to a King;
> Large petitions with thee bring,
> For His grace and power are such,
> None can ever ask too much. ~ John Newton

May this prayer of Spurgeon be personalized:

"O Jesus, by whom we come to God, seeing You have Yourself trodden the way of prayer, and never turned from it— teach me to remain a suppliant as long as I remain a sinner, and to wrestle in prayer so long as I have to wrestle with the powers of evil. Whatever else I may outgrow, may I never dream that I may relax my supplications."[561]

"Pray often, for prayer is a shield to the soul, a sacrifice to God, and a scourge to Satan."[562]

~ John Bunyan

[1] Needham, George C. *The Life and Labors of Charles H. Spurgeon.* (Boston: D. L. Guernsey, 1887), 7.

[2] Spurgeon, C. H. *An All-Round Ministry.* (Carlisle, PA: The Banner of Truth Trust, 1978).

[3] Bounds, E. M. *The Necessity of Prayer.* (New York: Revell, 1929), Chapter 4.

[4] Ryle, J. C. *Expository Thoughts on the Gospels: Luke,* Vol. 2. (Grand Rapids, MI: Baker Book House, 2007), 253.

[5] Davenport, Henry. *Life and Works of Charles H. Spurgeon.* (Memorial Publishing Co., 1892), 525–526.

[6] Murray, Andrew. *With Christ in the School of Prayer.* (New York: Revell), 6.

[7] Carson, D. A. "A Call to Spiritual Reformation: Priorities from Paul and His Prayers." (Baker Academic, 1992), 99.

[8] Courson, J. *Jon Courson's Application Commentary.* (Nashville, TN: Thomas Nelson, 2003), 941.

[9] https://deeperchristianquotes.com/prayer-is-laying-hold-of-gods-willingness-martin-luther/, accessed June 24, 2022.

[10] "What Prayer Is and Isn't." https://harvest.org/know-god-article/what-prayer-is-and-isnt/, accessed June 5, 2022.

[11] Blanchard, John. *Complete Gathered Gold.*

[12] Spurgeon, C. H. "A Poor Man's Cry, and What Came of It," sermon Delivered March 8, 1891.

[13] Kenyon, E. W. https://askgospel.com/e-w-kenyon-quotes/, accessed June 17, 2022.

[14] *Westminster Shorter Catechism,* Question 98.

[15] Rice, John R. *Prayer: Asking and Receiving.* (Murfreesboro, TN: Sword of the Lord Publishers, 1974), 48–49.

[16] Hodge, Charles. *Systematic Theology,* Vol. 3. (New York: Charles Scribner's Sons, 1884), 692.

[17] Cowman. *Streams in the Desert,* November 2.

[18] Stanley, Charles. *Walking With God.* (Atlanta, GA: In Touch Ministries, 2015), 136.

[19] Dixon, Francis. *Francis Dixon's Bible Study Notes, Studies in the Life of Elisha,* (Study #7).

[20] Watt, Gordon B. *Effectual Fervent Praye.r* (London: Marshall, Morgan & Scott, 1927), 140.

[21] Chadwick, Samuel. *The Path of Prayer.* (1931), Chapter 9.

[22] "The Mystery of Prayer," July 5, 1963. https://www.christianitytoday.com/ct/1963/july-5/layman-and-his-faith-mystery-of-prayer.html, accessed July 7, 2022. (Note: L. Nelson Bell was Billy Graham's father-in-law.)

[23] Chambers, Oswald. *Prayer: A Holy Occupation*. (Discovery House, 2010), 78.

[24] Trench, R. C. https://www.stresslesscountry.com/poemsaboutprayer.html, accessed June 24, 2022

[25] Plumer, W. S. *Studies in the Book of Psalms: Being a Critical and Expository Commentary, with Doctrinal and Practical Remarks on the Entire Psalter.* (Philadelphia; Edinburgh: J. B. Lippincott Company; A & C Black, 1872), 147.

[26] https://ministry127.com/resources/illustration/quotes-on-prayer, accessed June 26, 2022.

[27] Spurgeon, C. H. "Boldness at the Throne." Sermon delivered September 14, 1873, at the Metropolitan Tabernacle.

[28] Dixon, A. C. *Through Night to Morning*. (Greenville, SC: The Gospel Hour, Inc., no copyright date), Chapter 18.

[29] Pink, A. W. (2005). *The Lord's Prayer (Mt 6:9).* (Bellingham, WA: Logos Research Systems, Inc.).

[30] Bounds, E. M. The Complete Collection of E. M. Bounds on Prayer.

[31] Spurgeon, C. H. "Boldness at the Throne." Sermon delivered September 14, 1873, at the Metropolitan Tabernacle.

[32] https://www.thejesusgathering.org/watchman-nee.html

[33] https://prayer-coach.com/rc-sproul-quotes-prayer/, accessed June 28, 2022.

[34] Hallesby, Ole. *Prayer.* (London: Hodder & Stoughton, 1936).

[35] Ibid.

[36] Spurgeon, C. H. *An All-Around Ministry.* Chapter One.

[37] https://www.inspiringquotes.us/author/8177-f-b-meyer/about-prayer, accessed June 22, 2022.

[38] https://www.preceptaustin.org/prayer_quotes, accessed June 22, 2022.

[39] https://www.azquotes.com/quote/865135, accessed May 24, 2022.

[40] *Promises and Prayers for a Cherished Friend.* (Brentwood, TN: Freeman and Smith, 2012), 20.

[41] https://helpclubformoms.com/making-room-for-prayer

[42] Murray, Andrew. *God's Best Secrets.*

[43] Bounds, E. M. *Purpose in Prayer.* (New York: Revell, 1920), Chapter One.

[44] Moody, D. L. *Great Preaching on Prayer.* 8:119.

[45] Spurgeon, C. H. "Prayer—the Forerunner of Mercy," Sermon delivered June 28, 1857, at the Music Hall, Royal Surrey Gardens.

[46] https://wmpl.org/quote/, accessed May 26, 2018.

[47] Cowman, *Streams in the Desert,* October 2.

[48] Thomas A. Tarrants, https://www.cslewisinstitute.org/resources/why-pray/, accessed June 7, 2022.

[49] Keller, Tim. *Prayer: Experiencing Awe and Intimacy with God.* 68.

[50] Taken from "Answers to Prayer," from *George Müller's Narratives.*

[51] Spurgeon, C. H. *Morning and Evening.* October 18 (Morning).

[52] Thomas, W. H. G. *Life Abiding and Abounding: Bible Studies in Prayer and Meditation.* (Chicago: The Bible Institute Colportage Association, n.d.), 12.

[53] https://malaysiagospel.org/article/prayer-and-the-gospel

[54] https://cfaith.com/index.php/105-featured-c5-articles/21593-plead-your-case-3, accessed August 15, 2022.

[55] Bounds, E. M. *Purpose in Prayer.* (New York: Revell, 1920).

[56] *How to Live a Life of Prayer.* (Uhrichsville, Ohio: Barbour Books, 2018), 18.

[57] Ibid., 27.

[58] MacArthur, John. "The Plan of Prayer, Part 1" (Sermon), December 9, 1979.

[59] Towns, Elmer. *How to Pray.* (Ventura, Calif: Regal, 2006), 213.

[60] Morris, L. *The Gospel According to Matthew.* (Grand Rapids, MI; Leicester, England: W.B. Eerdmans; Inter-Varsity Press, 1992), 143.

[61] MacDonald, W. *Believer's Bible Commentary: Old and New Testaments,* (A. Farstad, Ed.). (Nashville: Thomas Nelson, 1995), 1224.

[62] Morris, L. *The Gospel According to Matthew.* (Grand Rapids, MI; Leicester, England: W.B. Eerdmans; Inter-Varsity Press, 1992), 143.

[63] Pink, A. W. & D. R. White. *A Guide to Fervent Prayer.* (Grand Rapids, MI: Baker Book House, 1981), 13.

[64] Spence-Jones, H. D. M. (Ed.). *St. Matthew* (Vol. 1). (London; New York: Funk & Wagnalls Company, 1909), 230.

[65] Spurgeon, C. H. *The New Park Street Pulpit Sermons* (Vol. 4) "The Fatherhood of God." (London; Glasgow: Passmore & Alabaster; James Paul; George John Stevenson; George Gallie, 1858), 385.

[66] Clarke, Adam. *Commentary on the Bible.* (1831), Matthew 6:9.

[67] Henry, M. *Matthew Henry's Commentary on the Whole Bible: Complete and Unabridged in One Volume.* (Peabody: Hendrickson, 1994), 1637.

[68] Ibid.

[69] Spurgeon, C. H. "Essential Points in Prayer," February 10, 1887.

[70] Henry, M. *Matthew Henry's Commentary on the Whole Bible: Complete and Unabridged in One Volume.* (Peabody: Hendrickson, 1994), 750.

[71] Pink, Arthur W. *An Exposition of The Sermon on the Mount.* (Grand Rapids, MI: Baker, 1950), 161–62.

[72] *King James Version Study Bible,* (electronic ed.). (Nashville: Thomas Nelson, 1997), Mt. 6:9.

[73] Pink, A. W. *The Lord's Prayer.* (Bellingham, WA: Logos Research Systems, Inc., 2005), Mt. 6:9.

[74] https://www.gty.org/library/sermons-library/2235/the-priority-of-prayer

[75] Pink, A. W. *The Lord's Prayer.* (Bellingham, WA: Logos Research Systems, Inc., 2005), Mt. 6:9.

[76] https://www.preceptaustin.org/prayer_quotes, accessed June 25 2022.

[77] Henry, M. *Matthew Henry's Commentary on the Whole Bible: Complete and Unabridged in One Volume.* (Peabody: Hendrickson, 1994), 1638.

[78] Stott, J. R. W. *The Message of the Sermon on the Mount (Matthew 5-7): Christian Counter-Culture.* (Leicester; Downers Grove, IL: InterVarsity Press, 1985), 147.

[79] https://johnstott.org/bible_studies/18-nov-2017/

[80] Stott, J. R. W. *The Message of the Sermon on the Mount (Matthew 5-7): Christian Counter-Culture.* (Leicester; Downers Grove, IL: InterVarsity Press, 1985), 149.

[81] Exell, J. S. *The Biblical Illustrator: Matthew.* (Grand Rapids, MI: Baker Book House, 1952), 96.

[82] Henry, M. *Matthew Henry's Commentary on the Whole Bible: Complete and Unabridged in One Volume.* (Peabody: Hendrickson, 1994), 1638.

[83] Exell, J. S. *The Biblical Illustrator: Matthew.* (Grand Rapids, MI: Baker Book House, 1952), 100.

[84] Ibid., 104.

[85] Pink, A. W. & D. R. White. *A Guide to Fervent Prayer.* (Grand Rapids, MI: Baker Book House, 1981), 13.

[86] Spurgeon, C. H. "True Prayer—True Power." Sermon Delivered August 12, 1860.

[87] Spurgeon, C. H. *2,200 Quotations: From the Writings of Charles H. Spurgeon: Arranged Topically or Textually and Indexed by Subject, Scripture, and People,* (T. Carter, Ed.). (Grand Rapids, MI: Baker Books, 1995), 145.

[88] Spurgeon, C. H. "Ejaculatory Prayer." Sermon delivered September 9, 1877.

[89] Stott, J. R. W. *The Message of the Sermon on the Mount (Matthew 5-7): Christian Counter-Culture.* (Leicester; Downers Grove, IL: InterVarsity Press, 1985), 147.

[90] Spurgeon, C. H. "Behold, He Prayeth." Sermon Delivered September 20, 1885.

[91] Ibid.

[92] Ibid.

[93] Ibid.

[94] Spurgeon, C. H. "Essential Points in Prayer," Sermon Delivered February 10, 1887.

[95] McIntyre, David M. *The Hidden Life of Prayer.*

[96] Spurgeon, C. H. *Flowers from a Puritan's Garden.* (New York: Funk & Wagnalls, 1883).

[97] McIntyre, David M. *The Hidden Life of Prayer.*

[98] Hallesby, Ole. *Prayer.* (Minneapolis, Minnesota: Augsburg Publishing House, 1931), 5.

[99] Chadwick, Samuel. *Path to Pray.* (1931), Chapter 9.

[100] https://www.azquotes.com/quote/712458, accessed June 25, 2022.

[101] https://www.azquotes.com/quote/544823?ref=affair

[102] Zodhiates, S. *The Complete Word Study Dictionary: New Testament* (electronic ed.). (Chattanooga, TN: AMG Publishers, 2000).

[103] https://prayer-coach.com/prayer-quotes-andrew-murray/

[104] Spence-Jones, H. D. M. (Ed.). *St. Matthew* (Vol. 1). (London; New York: Funk & Wagnalls Company, 1909), 242.

[105] Spurgeon, C. H. *Psalms.* (Wheaton, IL: Crossway Books, 1993), 271.

[106] https://www.preceptaustin.org/prayer_quotes, accessed June 15, 2022.

[107] https://www.azquotes.com/quote/550390, accessed June 23, 2022.

[108] Clarke, Adam. *Christian Theology.* (1835), 252.

[109] Hallesby, Ole. *Prayer.* (Minneapolis, Minnesota: Augsburg Publishing House, 1931), 48.

[110] Torrey, R. A. *How to Pray.* (Chicago; New York: Fleming H. Revell Company, 1900), 33–34.

[111] Tozer, A. W. "Courageous Prayer." Tozer Devotional, February 11, 2013, http://www.cmalliance.org/devotions/tozer?id=822, accessed October 4, 2014.

[112] https://prayer-coach.com/tim-keller-prayer-quotes/

[113] Spurgeon, C. H. *Flowers from a Puritan's Garden.* (New York: Funk & Wagnalls, 1883), 249.

[114] Wiersbe, Warren W. *The Names of Jesus.*

[115] https://christlifemin.org/assets/pdf/Prayer_O_Hallesby.pdf.

[116] Hutson, Curtis. *Great Preaching on Prayer,* 112.

[117] Hallesby, Ole. *Prayer.* (Minneapolis, Minnesota: Augsburg Publishing House, 1931), 28.

[118] Spurgeon, C. H. *Flowers from a Puritan's Garden.* (New York: Funk & Wagnalls, 1883), 249.

[119] https://christlifemin.org/2022/05/29/the-prayer-for-revival/

[120] Spurgeon, C. H. "The Holy Spirit's Intercession." Sermon delivered April 11, 1880.

[121] Exell, J. S. *The Biblical Illustrator: Romans* (Vol. 2). (New York; Chicago; Toronto; London; Edinburgh: Fleming H. Revell Company, n.d.), 143.

[122] Exell, J. S. *The Biblical Illustrator: Ephesians.* (New York; Chicago; Toronto; London; Edinburgh: Fleming H. Revell Company, n.d.), 684.

[123] "How to Pray in the Spirit." https://www.lwf.org/sermons/audio/how-to-pray-in-the-spirit-0520, accessed June 8, 2022.

[124] Hindson, E. E., and W. M. Kroll, (Eds.). *KJV Bible Commentary.* (Nashville: Thomas Nelson, 1994), 1894.

[125] MacArthur, J., Jr. (Ed.). *The MacArthur Study Bible* (electronic ed.). (Nashville, TN: Word Pub., 1997), 1402.

[126] Spurgeon, C. H. *Lectures to My Students.* (Grand Rapids: Zondervan Publishing House, 1970), 55–56.

[127] Spence-Jones, H. D. M. (Ed.). *Ecclesiastes.* (London; New York: Funk & Wagnalls Company, 1909), 111.

[128] Henry, M. *Matthew Henry's Commentary on the Whole Bible: Complete and Unabridged in One Volume.* (Peabody: Hendrickson, 1994), 1039.

[129] Chadwick, Samuel. *Path to Prayer.* (1931), Chapter 2.

[130] https://www.preceptaustin.org/prayer_quotes, accessed June 15, 2022.

[131] McIntyre, David M. *The Hidden Life of Prayer.*

[132] Torrey, R. A. *How to Pray.* (Chicago; New York: Fleming H. Revell Company, 1900), 12.

[133] Henry, M. *Matthew Henry's Commentary on the Whole Bible: Complete and Unabridged in One Volume.* (Peabody: Hendrickson, 1994), 563.

[134] Spurgeon, C. H. "The Prayer of Jabez." In *The Metropolitan Tabernacle Pulpit Sermons,* (Vol. 17). (London: Passmore & Alabaster, 1871), 314.

[135] Ibid.

[136] Henry, M. *Matthew Henry's Commentary on the Whole Bible: Complete and Unabridged in One Volume.* (Peabody: Hendrickson, 1994), 563.

[137] Bonar, Andrew. *Memoir and Remains of the Rev. Robert Murray M'Cheyne, Minister of St. Peter's Church, Dundee.* (1852), 160.

[138] https://prayer-coach.com/prayer-quotes-jim-cymbala/

[139] Hutson, Curtis, (ed.). *Great Preaching on Comfort.* (Murfreesboro, TN: Sword of the Lord Publishers, 1990), 122.

[140] Jeremiah, David. Blog. "4 Questions Answered on the Importance of Prayer." https:// davidjeremiah.blog/4-questions-answered-on-the-importance-of-prayer/, accessed July 24, 2020.

[141] https://graciousquotes.com/prayer/ https://www.preceptaustin.org/prayer_quotes_devotionals_illustrations

[142] Stott, John. *The Letters of John.* (Tyndale New Testament Commentaries," rev. ed.). (Leicester: IVP, 1988), 188.

[143] Courson, J. *Jon Courson's Application Commentary.* (Nashville, TN: Thomas Nelson, 2003), 193.

[144] Blackaby, Henry. *Experiencing God,* 194

[145] https://www.preceptaustin.org/prayer_quotes, accessed June15, 2022.

[146] "What Is Prayer and Why Do We Pray?," https://www.lwf.org/who-is-god-what-is-he-like/what-is-prayer-and-why-do-we-pray, accessed June 5, 2022.

[147] Spurgeon, C. H. "Comfort for Those Whose Prayers Are Feeble," Sermon From the May 1872 Sword and Trowel.

[148] Rice, John R. "Prevailing Prayer Requires Faith," cited in *Great Preaching on Prayer.* (Murfreesboro, TN: Sword of the Lord Publishers, 1988), 115.

[149] Spurgeon, C. H. *2,200 Quotations: from the Writings of Charles H. Spurgeon: Arranged Topically or Textually and Indexed by Subject, Scripture, and People, (T. Carter, Ed.).* (Grand Rapids, MI: Baker Books, 1995), 143.

[150] Criswell, W. A. "The Perfect Fellowship." Sermon Delivered February 27, 1977, First Baptist Church, Dallas, Texas.

[151] https://www.christianquotes.info/top-quotes/22-motivating-quotes-about-prayer/, accessed June 23, 2022.

[152] https://www.azquotes.com/quote/943384

[153] https://www.preceptaustin.org/prayer_quotes, accessed June 15, 2022.

[154] https://www.preceptaustin.org/prayer_quotes, accessed June 15, 2022.

[155] https://prayer-coach.com/prayer-quotes-andrew-murray/

[156] https://www.azquotes.com/quote/1211217

[157] Spurgeon, C. H. "Essential Points in Prayer," Delivered February 10, 1887.

[158] Harman, A. *Psalms: A Mentor Commentary* (Vol. 1–2). (Ross-shire, Great Britain: Mentor, 2011), 117.

[159] Cited in Leonard Ravenhill, *Heart Cry for Revival*. (Grand Rapids: Zondervan, 1969), 78.

[160] Aquinas, Thomas. Paul Murray, *Praying with Confidence: Aquinas on the Lord's Prayer.*

[161] Ibid.

[162] Spurgeon, C. H. "Pray Without Ceasing." Sermon Delivered March 10, 1872. *Metropolitan Tabernacle Pulpit,* Volume 18.

[163] Spurgeon, C. H. *Psalms.* (Wheaton, IL: Crossway Books, 1993), 109.

[164] Hallesby, Ole. *Prayer.* (Minneapolis, Minnesota: Augsburg Publishing House, 1931), 77.

[165] Spurgeon, C. H. *Psalms.* (Wheaton, IL: Crossway Books, 1993), 19.

[166] Kirkpatrick, A. F. Psalm 28:2.

[167] Harman, A. *Psalms: A Mentor Commentary* (Vol. 1–2). (Ross-shire, Great Britain: Mentor, 2011), 252.

[168] *Ellicott's Commentary for English Readers*, 1 Timothy 2:8.

[169] Spurgeon, C. H. *Psalms.* (Wheaton, IL: Crossway Books, 1993), 109.

[170] *Maclaren's Expositions*, 1 Timothy 2:8.

[171] *Barnes Notes on the Bible*, 1 Timothy 2:8.

[172] *Gill's Exposition of the Entire Bible*, 1 Timothy 2:8.

[173] Bounds, E. M. *Power Through Prayer*, "Deliberation Necessary to Largest Results from Prayer," Chapter 19.

[174] https://www.allchristianquotes.org/topics/5356/hurry/, accessed May 24, 2022.

[175] Olford, Stephen. *Basics For Believers*. (Colorado Springs, CO: Victor, 2003), 287.

[176] Watt, Gordon B. *Effectual Fervent Prayer*. (London: Marshall, Morgan & Scott, 1927), 40.

[177] Spurgeon, C. H. *Sermons on Prayer,* Sermon: "Where True Prayer is Found." (London: Marshall, Morgan & Scott, 1962), 35.

[178] *How to Live a Life of Prayer,* 158.

[179] Watt, Gordon B. *Effectual Fervent Prayer*. (London: Marshall, Morgan & Scott, 1927), 140.

[180] Ibid.

[181] *The Christian Pioneer,* Volumes 29–31. (London: Simpkin, Marshall & Company, 1875), 9.

[182] Spurgeon, Charles Haddon. *Spurgeon at His Best: Over 2,200 Striking Quotations from the World's Most Exhaustive and Widely Read Sermon Series.* (Baker Publishing Group, 1988).

[183] Spurgeon, C. H. "True Prayer—True Power." Sermon Delivered August 12, 1860.

[184] Cowman, *Streams in the Desert,* March 24. (no reference cited)

[185] Shaw, Harold. *George Müller: Delighted in God!,* (1975), 310.

[186] Hallesby, Ole. *Prayer.* (Minneapolis, Minnesota: Augsburg Publishing House, 1931), 58.

[187] Bounds, E. M. *The Necessity of Prayer.* (New York: Revell, 1929).

[188] Cymbala, Jim. *Fresh Wind Fresh Fire: What Happens When God's Spirit Invades the Hearts of His People.* (2010), 70.

[189] Chadwick, Samuel. *The Path of Prayer.* (Kansas City: Beacon Hill, 1931).

[190] Courson, J. *Jon Courson's Application Commentary.* (Nashville, TN: Thomas Nelson, 2003), 1153–1154.

[191] Parsons, Charles R. *An Hour with George Müller: The Man of Faith to Whom God Gave Millions.*

[192] Packer, J. I. *The J. I. Packer Classic Collection.* (Colorado Springs: NavPress, 2010), 223.

[193] Spurgeon, C. H. A Poor Man's Cry, and What Came of It, sermon Delivered March 8, 1891.

[194] Duewel, Wesley. *Mighty Prevailing Prayer: Experiencing the Power of Answered Prayer.* (Grand Rapids, MI: Zondervan, 1990), 17.

[195] Spurgeon, C. H. "True Prayer—True Power." Sermon delivered August 12, 1860.

[196] Spurgeon, C. H. *Flowers from a Puritan's Garden.* (New York: Funk & Wagnalls, 1883), 38–39.

[197] Exell, J. S. *The Biblical Illustrator: The Psalms,* Vol. 2. (New York; Chicago; Toronto; London; Edinburgh: Fleming H. Revell Company), 46.

[198] Spurgeon, C. H. *Flowers from a Puritan's Garden.* (New York: Funk & Wagnalls, 1883), 172–173.

[199] https://prayer-coach.com/prayer-quote-billy-graham/, accessed July 15 2022.

[200] Hughes, R. Kent. *The Sermon on the Mount: The Message of the Kingdom.* (2013), Chapter 23.

[201] "What Is Prayer and Why Do We Pray?," https://www.lwf.org/who-is-god-what-is-he-like/what-is-prayer-and-why-do-we-pray, accessed May 25, 2022.

[202] Hayford, Jack. *Prayer Is Invading The Impossible.* (Plainfield, NJ: Logos, 1977), 97.

[203] Chambers, Oswald. "Prayer: A Holy Occupation."

[204] Spurgeon, C. H. *Flowers from a Puritan's Garden.* (New York: Funk & Wagnalls, 1883), 35.

[205] "What Is Prayer and Why Do We Pray?," https://www.lwf.org/who-is-god-what-is-he-like/what-is-prayer-and-why-do-we-pray, accessed May 25, 2022.

[206] https://www.crosswalk.com/faith/spiritual-life/inspiring-quotes/31-prayer-quotes-be-inspired-and-encouraged.html, accessed May 24, 2022.

[207] Criswell, W. A. "Getting Things from God," sermon delivered Sunday morning, October 27, 1974.

[208] Wiersbe, W. W. *The Bible Exposition Commentary* (Vol. 1). (Wheaton, IL: Victor Books, 1996, 26.

[209] https://www.preceptaustin.org/prayer_quotes, accessed June 15, 2022.

[210] Bounds, E. M. *The Necessity of Prayer.* (New York: Revell, 1929).

[211] Barnes, Albert. *Notes on the Bible.* (1834), James 5:16.

[212] Spurgeon, C. H. "Prayer Meetings," Sermon delivered August 30, 1868, Metropolitan Tabernacle.

[213] Spurgeon, C. H. *Morning and Evening,* January 15.

[214] https://www.preceptaustin.org/prayer_quotes, accessed Jun 15, 2022.

[215] Ryle, J. C. "A Call to Prayer." www.gracegems.org, accessed May 9, 2017.

[216] https://www.spurgeongems.org/sermon/chs3344.pdf

[217] https://www.azquotes.com/author/18668-Thomas_Brooks/tag/prayer, accessed May 22, 2022.

[218] Bounds, E. M. *The Necessity of Prayer.* (New York: Revell, 1929), Chapter IV.

[219] Ibid.

[220] McNaughton, I. S. *Opening Up Colossians and Philemon.* (Leominster: Day One Publications, 2006), 93.

[221] Courson, J. *Jon Courson's Application Commentary.* (Nashville, TN: Thomas Nelson, 2003), 1327–1328.

[222] https://www.azquotes.com/quote/544969.

[223] Henry, M. *Matthew Henry's Commentary on the Whole Bible: Complete and Unabridged in One Volume.* (Peabody: Hendrickson, 1994), 2337.

[224] Chadwick, Samuel. *Path to Prayer.* (1931), Chapter 9.

[225] https://www.morefamousquotes.com/topics/quotes-about-wrestling-with-god/, accessed June 26, 2022.

[226] Hallesby, Ole. *Prayer.* (London: Hodder & Stoughton, 1936).

[227] https://www.azquotes.com/quote/935524.

[228] Maclaren, Alexander. *The Book of Psalms,* 171.

[229] Bishop Hall. Exell, J. S., (Ed.). *The Biblical Illustrator: St. Luke* (Vol. II). (London: James Nisbet & Co., n.d.), 313.

[230] Cowman, L. B. *Streams in the Desert.* (Grand Rapids: Zondervan, 1997), April 24.

[231] https://www.preceptaustin.org/prayer_quotes, accessed June 15, 2022.

[232] Ibid.

[233] Ibid., accessed June 24, 2022.

[234] McConkey, James H. *Prayer.*

[235] https://www.preceptaustin.org/prayer_quotes, accessed June 15, 2022.

[236] Cowman, L. B. *Streams in the Desert.* (Grand Rapids: Zondervan, 1997), 314–315.

[237] Bounds, E. M. *The Necessity of Prayer.* (New York: Revell, 1929).

[238] Spurgeon, C. H. "Growth in Grace" (Sermon delivered October 17, 1858). https://www.spurgeon.org/resource-library/sermons/growth-in-grace/#flipbook/, accessed June 3, 2021.

[239] McConkey, James H. *Prayer.* (Pittsburgh: Silver Publishing Company, 1931), 69.

[240] Spurgeon, C. H. *Sermons on Prayer.* Sermon: "Opening The Mouth." (London: Marshall, Morgan, & Scott, 1962), 99.

[241] Spurgeon, C. H. "True Prayer—True Power." Sermon delivered August 12, 1860.

[242] Spurgeon, C. H. "The Secret of Power in Prayer," Sermon delivered January 8, 1888 at the Metropolitan Tabernacle.

[243] Tozer, A. W. *Man—The Dwelling Place of God,* Chapter 21.

[244] Rice, John R. *Prayer—Asking and Receiving.* (Murfreesboro, TN: Sword of the Lord Publishers, 1942), Chapter 19.

[245] Blanchard, John. *Complete Gathered Gold.*

[246] Henry, M. *Matthew Henry's Commentary on the Whole Bible: Complete and Unabridged in One Volume.* (Peabody: Hendrickson, 1994), James 4.

[247] Hayford, Jack. *Prayer Is Invading the Impossible.* (2001), 154.

[248] https://www.christianquotes.info/quotes-by-topic/quotes-about-intercession/, accessed June 17, 2022.

[249] Spurgeon, C. H. "Yield Fully to the Holy Spirit," cited in *Herald of His Coming,* (May/June 2022), 6.

[250] Lloyd-Jones, Martyn. *Preaching and Preachers.* (Hachette, UK, 2012), 90.

[251] Finney, Charles. *Letters On Revival:* No. 12, July 2, 1845.

[252] https://www.azquotes.com/quote/545019

[253] Hallesby, Ole. *Prayer.* (Minneapolis, Minnesota: Augsburg Publishing House, 1931), 46.

[254] https://gracequotes.org/author-quote/andrew-bonar/

[255] https://gracequotes.org/topic/prayer-satan/

[256] Ryle, J. C. *Expository Thoughts on the Gospels: Luke,* Vol. 2. (Grand Rapids, MI: Baker Book House, 2007), 253.

[257] https://biblereasons.com/distractions/

[258] Hallesby, Ole. *Prayer.* (Augsburg Fortress Publishing, 1975).

[259] Rees, Paul S. https://place.asburyseminary.edu/cgi/viewcontent.cgi?article=2133&context=asburyjournal

[260] Spurgeon, C. H. "Comfort for Those Whose Prayers Are Feeble." Sermon delivered at The Metropolitan Tabernacle, published March 12, 1908.

[261] Spurgeon, C. H. "The Sealed Hand—A Winter Sermon." Sermon published on Thursday, February 15, 1912.

[262] Hallesby, Ole. *Prayer.* (Minneapolis, Minnesota: Augsburg Publishing House, 1931), 20.

[263] Spurgeon, C. H. "The Amen." Sermon delivered March 4, 1866, Metropolitan Tabernacle.

[264] Chalmers, Alexander. *The Table Talk of Martin Luther.* (1857), 102.

[265] Spurgeon, C. H. "The Amen." Sermon delivered March 4, 1866, Metropolitan Tabernacle.

[266] Ibid.

[267] Tozer, A. W. *The Next Chapter After the Last: For the Child of God, the Best Is Yet to Come.* (Chicago: Moody Publishers, 1987), Chapter 24.

[268] Bounds, E. M. *How to Live a Life of Prayer.* (Uhrichsville, Ohio: Barbour Books, 2018), 130.

[269] Cowman. *Streams in the Desert,* October 26.

[270] Spurgeon, C. H. *Flowers from a Puritan's Garden.* (New York: Funk & Wagnalls, 1883), 172.

[271] Henry, M. *Matthew Henry's Commentary on the Whole Bible: Complete and Unabridged in One Volume.* (Peabody: Hendrickson, 1994), 1637.

[272] Spurgeon, C. H. *Lectures to My Students.* (Grand Rapids, MI: Zondervan, 1970), 43.

[273] https://www.revival-library.org/prayer_makes_history/ hyde_john.shtml, accessed June 24, 2022.

[274] Henry, M. *Matthew Henry's Commentary on the Whole Bible: Complete and Unabridged in One Volume.* (Peabody: Hendrickson, 1994), 1757.

[275] Sproul, R. C. *Does Prayer Change Things?*

[276] Spurgeon, C. H. *Lectures to My Students.* (Grand Rapids: Zondervan Publishing House, 1970), 61.

[277] à Kempis, Thomas. *Christian Classics in Modern English: The Imitation of Christ.* (Wheaton. IL: Harold Shaw Publishers, 1991), 78.

[278] Cited in the *Baltimore & Ohio Railroad Magazine,* (January 1936,) 63.

[279] https://www.preceptaustin.org/prayer_quotes, accessed August 5, 2022.

[280] https://prayer-coach.com/tim-keller-prayer-quotes/

[281] https://www.azquotes.com/quote/870695

[282] https://www.allchristianquotes.org/quotes/Charles_G_Finney/553/

[283] Duewel, Wesley L. *Touch the World Through Prayer.* (Zondervan, 1986), 23.

[284] Spurgeon, C. H. *Flowers from a Puritan's Garden.* (New York: Funk & Wagnalls, 1883), 175.

[285] Exell, J. S. *The Biblical Illustrator: Matthew.* (Grand Rapids, MI: Baker Book House, 1952), 409.

[286] Torrey, R. A. *How to Pray.* (Chicago; New York: Fleming H. Revell Company, 1900), 38.

[287] Müller, George. *The Autobiography of George Müller.* (1984), 47–48.

[288] Cited in the autobiography of Clarence E. MacCartney (adapted for use here).

[289] Spurgeon, C. H. *Flowers from a Puritan's Garden.* (New York: Funk & Wagnalls, 1883), 176.

[290] Sweeting, George. *Who Said That?: More than 2,500 Usable Quotes and Illustrations,* under heading of Prayer.

[291] *Christian History,* 25.

[292] https://www.preceptaustin.org/prayer_quotes, accessed June 25, 20222.

[293] Spurgeon, C. H. *Lectures to My Students.* (Grand Rapids: Zondervan Publishing House, 1970), 57.

[294] Ibid., 56.

[295] Wiersbe, W. W. *Wiersbe's Expository Outlines on the New Testament.* (Wheaton, IL: Victor Books, 1992), 32.

[296] Spurgeon, C. H. *Lectures to My Students.* (Grand Rapids: Zondervan Publishing House, 1970), 55.

[297] Ibid., 60.

[298] Ibid., 68.

[299] Ibid.

[300] Ibid., 59.

[301] *The Prayer Meeting and Its History.* (Pittsburgh: United Presbyterian Board of Publication, 1870).

[302] Ibid.

[303] https://wmpl.org/quote/since-the-days-of-pentecost/, accessed July 18, 2022.

[304] Spurgeon, C. H. "A Call to Worship," Sermon delivered April 19, 1873.

[305] Spurgeon suggests a cure. "A good cure for this evil is for the minister judiciously to admonish the brother to study brevity, and if this avail not, to jog his elbow when the people are getting weary." *Only a Prayer Meeting,* 17.

[306] J. F. Cowan. *More Prayer in the Prayer Meeting.* (New York, 1906).

[307] *The Institute Tie.* (Chicago, Ill., September, 1900), 83.

[308] Spence-Jones, H. D. M. (Ed.). *St. Matthew* (Vol. 2). (London; New York: Funk & Wagnalls Company, 1909), 227.

[309] Murray, Andrew. *The Ministry of Intercessory Prayer.*

[310] Spurgeon, C. H. "Paul's First Prayer," a Sermon delivered March 25, 1855, at Exeter Hall, London.

[311] Whitney, Donald S. *Spiritual Disciplines of the Christian Life.* (Colorado Springs: NavPress, 1991), 164.

[312] Ibid., 160.

[313] Chambers, *My Utmost for His Highest,* July 17.

314 Whitney, Donald S. *Spiritual Disciplines of the Christian Life.* (Colorado Springs: NavPress, 1991), 160.

315 https://www.christianquotes.info/quotes-by-topic/quotes-about-fasting/, accessed June 25, 2022.

316 *Matthew Henry's Whole Bible Commentary,* Zechariah 7:1.

317 Bright, Bill. *Your Personal Guide to Fasting and Prayer.*

318 Nolland, J. *The Gospel of Matthew: A Commentary on the Greek Text.* (Grand Rapids, MI: Carlisle; W. B. Eerdmans; Paternoster Press, 2005), 276.

319 Redpath, Alan. *Victorious Christian Service.* (Old Tappan, NJ: Fleming H. Revell Company, 1958), 23.

320 Watt, Gordon B. *Effectual Fervent Prayer.* (London: Marshall, Morgan & Scott, 1927), 17.

321 Bounds, E. M. *Prayer and Spiritual Warfare,* 113.

322 From Ryle, J. C., "A Call to Prayer." https://www.goodreads.com/quotes/8443868-there-is-a-way-by-which-any-person-however-sinful, accessed June 26, 2020.

323 Henry, M. *Matthew Henry's Commentary on the Whole Bible: Complete and Unabridged in One Volume.* (Peabody: Hendrickson, 1994), 1857.

324 Gordon, S. D.

325 Watt, Gordon B. *Effectual Fervent Prayer.* (London: Marshall, Morgan & Scott, 1927), 25.

326 Rogers, Adrian. "Prayer and the Will of God" (Sermon), https://www.lightsource.com/ministry/love-worth-finding/articles/prayer-and-the-will-of-god-12760.html, accessed July 1, 2022.

327 Bounds, E. M. *The Weapon of Prayer,* 8.

328 Watt, Gordon B. *Effectual Fervent Prayer.* (London: Marshall, Morgan & Scott, 1927), 66.

329 Prime, Derek. *Practical Prayer: The Why and How of Prayer.* (Focus Publishing).

330 Watt, Gordon B. *Effectual Fervent Prayer.* (London: Marshall, Morgan & Scott, 1927), 19.

331 Storms, Sam. "How to Pray Against Satan," January 28, 2020. https://www.desiringgod.org/articles/how-to-pray-against-satan, accessed July 2, 2022.

332 https://gracequotes.org/author-quote/david-brainerd/

333 https://www.spiritualwarfare.blog/various-quotes

[334] Spurgeon, C. H. *2,200 Quotations: From the Writings of Charles H. Spurgeon: Arranged Topically or Textually and Indexed by Subject, Scripture, and People,* (T. Carter, Ed.). (Grand Rapids, MI: Baker Books, 1995), 149.

[335] https://www.scribd.com/book/278226106/A-Year-of-Prayer-Growing-Closer-to-God-Week-After-Week

[336] https://prayer-coach.com/prayer-quotes-oswald-chambers/, accessed July 15, 2022.

[337] Spurgeon, C. H. "Ejaculatory Prayer," Sermon delivered September 9, 1877.

[338] Ibid.

[339] https://www.azquotes.com/quote/664906, accessed July 26, 2022.

[340] https://www.goodreads.com/quotes/323811-satan-dreads-nothing-but-prayer-his-one-concern-is-to. Accessed June 20, 2022.

[341] Dixon, Francis. "The Sin of Prayerlessness," Study 2, Series 57. (Words of Life Ministries).

[342] Bounds, E. M. *The Complete Collection of E. M. Bounds on Prayer.*

[343] https://www.worldinvisible.com/library/murray/praylife/prayer01.htm

[344] https://www.azquotes.com/quote/874582

[345] Wiersbe, Warren W., David W. Wiersbe. *10 Power Principles for Christian Service.* (Grand Rapids: Baker Books, 2010), 86.

[346] Nee, Watchman. *The Finest of the Wheat,* vol. 2—Hardcover: *Selected Excerpts from the Published Works of Watchman Nee.* (Christian Fellowship Publishers, 1993), 66.

[347] https://slideplayer.com/slide/13104674/

[348] Hallesby, Ole. *Prayer.* (London: Hodder & Stoughton, 1936).

[349] *A Puritan Golden Treasury,* compiled by Thomas, I. D. E., by permission of Banner of Truth, Carlisle, Pa., 2000, 211.

[350] https://www.princeofpreachers.org/quotable-quotes.html, accessed July 26, 2022.

[351] https://www.embounds.online/prayer-quotes

[352] Taylor, Jack. *Prayer: Life's Limitless Reach.* (Nashville: Broadman, 1977).

[353] https://gracequotes.org/author-quote/d-l-moody/

[354] https://billygrahamlibrary.org/preparing-for-evangelistic-outreach/

[355] Spurgeon, C. H. *Flowers from a Puritan's Garden.* (New York: Funk & Wagnalls, 1883), 56.

[356] https://prayer-coach.com/prayer-quotes-andrew-murray/

[357] Carson, D. A. *A Call to Spiritual Reformation: Priorities from Paul and His Prayers.* (Baker Academic, 1992), 29.

[358] Hallesby, Ole. *Prayer.* (Minneapolis, Minnesota: Augsburg Publishing House, 1931), 41–42.

[359] Bounds, E. M. *Preacher and Prayer.* (Nashville: House of the M.E. Church, 1907), 30.

[360] https://www.preceptaustin.org/prayer_quotes, accessed June 15, 2022.

[361] Plumer, W. S. *Studies in the Book of Psalms: Being a Critical and Expository Commentary, with Doctrinal and Practical Remarks on the Entire Psalter.* (Philadelphia; Edinburgh: J. B. Lippincott Company; A & C Black, 1872), 89.

[362] Murray, Andrew. *God's Best Secrets.*

[363] https://www.allchristianquotes.org/quotes/Martin_Luther/1688/

[364] Exell, J. S. *The Biblical Illustrator: Ephesians.* (New York; Chicago; Toronto; London; Edinburgh: Fleming H. Revell Company, n.d.), 682.

[365] Spurgeon, Susannah and William Harrald. *Autobiography, Diary, Letters, and Records,* Vol. 1, 172

[366] Parsons, Charles R. *An Hour with George Müller: The Man of Faith to Whom God Gave Millions.*

[367] McIntyre, David M. *The Hidden Life of Prayer,* Chapter 6.

[368] Rogers, Adrian. "Prayer and the Will of God," (Sermon), https://www.lightsource.com/ministry/love-worth-finding/articles/prayer-and-the-will-of-god-12760.html, accessed July 1, 2022.

[369] Spurgeon, C. H. "Pray Without Ceasing," Sermon Delivered March 10, 1872. *Metropolitan Tabernacle Pulpit,* Volume 18.

[370] *Metropolitan Tabernacle Pulpit,* 49:476.

[371] Merkle, B. L. *Ephesians,* (2018). In I. M. Duguid, J. M. Hamilton Jr., and J. Sklar (Eds.). *Ephesians–Philemon* (Vol. XI,(Wheaton, IL: Crossway), 115.

[372] *Barnes Notes on the Bible,* 1 Thessalonians 5:17.

[373] Jeremiah, David. "Spiritual Warfare Prayer." https://davidjeremiah.blog/spiritual-warfare-prayer/, accessed June 30, 2022.

[374] MacArthur, J., Jr. (Ed.). *The MacArthur Study Bible* (electronic ed.). (Nashville, TN: Word Pub., 1997), 1850.

[375] Spence-Jones, H. D. M. (Ed.). *1 Thessalonians.* (London; New York: Funk & Wagnalls Company, 1909), 105.

[376] https://www.preceptaustin.org/prayer_quotes, accessed June 15, 2022.

[377] https://www.biblia.work/sermons/prayermethod-of/, accessed June 25, 2022.

[378] Spurgeon, C. H. "The Importunate Widow," sermon delivered February 21, 1869.

[379] Barnes, Albert. *Notes on the Bible.* (1834), Luke 18:7.

[380] https://www.preceptaustin.org/prayer_quotes, accessed June 15, 2022.

[381] Bounds, E. M. *Prayer and Spiritual Warfare,* 115.

[382] https://prayer-coach.com/prayer-quote-billy-graham/, accessed July 15, 2022.

[383] MacArthur, John. *Alone With God: Rediscovering the Power and Passion of Prayer.* (Colorado Springs, CO: Victor, 1995), 16.

[384] Exell, J. S. *The Biblical Illustrator: Thessalonians,* (Vol. 1). (New York; Chicago; Toronto: Fleming H. Revell Company, n.d.), 239.

[385] Ibid.

[386] https://www.azquotes.com/author/22604-Woodrow_M_Kroll, accessed June 25, 2022.

[387] https://www.christianquotes.info/images/3-reasons-always-pray/

[388] *Matthew Henry's Concise Commentary,* Jeremiah 33:3.

[389] *Encounter Weekly,* 1996. http://www.tentmaker.org/Quotes/prayerquotes.htm, accessed December 25, 2013.

[390] Criswell, W. A. "Getting Things from God," sermon Delivered Sunday morning, October 27, 1974.

[391] Ravenhill, Leonard. *Why Revival Tarries.* (Minneapolis, MN: Bethany House, 1987), 119.

[392] Spence-Jones, H. D. M. (Ed.). *St. Mark* (Vol. 2). (London; New York: Funk & Wagnalls Company, 1909), 24.

[393] https://prayer-coach.com/prayer-quote-billy-graham/, accessed July 15, 2022.

[394] https://www.goodreads.com/author/quotes/3317101, accessed June 27, 2022,

[395] Moody, D. L. *Prevailing Prayer: What Hinders It?* (Chicago: Revell, 1884), 4.

[396] Bonhoeffer, Dietrich in Samuel Wells. *Life Together.* (SCM Press, 2015), 35.

[397] https://quotlr.com/quotes-about-meditation-and-prayer, accessed June 27, 2022.

[398] From the *Autobiography of George Müller,* May 9, 1841.

[399] Bounds, E. M. *The Necessity of Prayer.* (New York: Revell, 1929).

[400] Spurgeon, C. H. "The Secret of Power in Prayer," Sermon delivered January 8, 1888 at the Metropolitan Tabernacle.

[401] Exell, J. S. *The Biblical Illustrator: Ephesians.* (New York; Chicago; Toronto; London; Edinburgh: Fleming H. Revell Company, n.d.), 627.

[402] O'Brien, P. T. *The Letter to the Ephesians.* (Grand Rapids, MI: W.B. Eerdmans Publishing Co., 1999), 462.

[403] Lloyd-Jones, Martyn. *The Christian Soldier.* (Grand Rapids: Baker, 1977), 179.

[404] MacIntyre, David. *The Hidden Life of Prayer,* Chapter 6: The Engagement: Request.

[405] Exell, J. S. *The Biblical Illustrator: Ephesians.* (New York; Chicago; Toronto; London; Edinburgh: Fleming H. Revell Company, n.d.), 683. Adapted.

[406] Plumer, W. S. *Studies in the Book of Psalms: Being a Critical and Expository Commentary, with Doctrinal and Practical Remarks on the Entire Psalter.* (Philadelphia; Edinburgh: J. B. Lippincott Company; A & C Black, 1872), 79–80.

[407] Ibid., 89.

[408] Maclaren, Alexander. *The Book of Psalms,* Psalm 5:3.

[409] Pierson, A. T. *George Müller of Bristol: His Life of Prayer and Faith.* (Grand Rapids: Kregel Publishing, 1999), 73.

[410] Spurgeon, C. H. "The Golden Key of Prayer," Sermon delivered March 12, 1865, Metropolitan Tabernacle.

[411] https://www.crosswalk.com/faith/spiritual-life/inspiring-quotes/31-prayer-quotes-be-inspired-and-encouraged.html, accessed May 24, 2022.

[412] https://ccel.org/ccel/bounds/purpose/purpose.I_1.html

[413] https://www.preceptaustin.org/prayer_quotes, accessed June 24, 2022.

[414] Ibid., accessed June 15, 2022.

[415] Hallesby, Ole. *Prayer.* (London: Hodder & Stoughton, 1936).

[416] Bright, Bill. (Ed.). *Ten Steps Toward Christian Maturity Teacher's Manual.* (Arrowhead Springs, CA: Campus Crusade for Christ, International, 1965), 228.

[417] https://biblereasons.com/prayer-quotes/, accessed May 20, 2022.

[418] https://www.azquotes.com/author/14750-Aiden_Wilson_Tozer, accessed August 25, 2021.

[419] Bounds, E. M. *How to Live a Life of Prayer.* (Uhrichsville, Ohio: Barbour Books, 2018), 50.

[420] Chadwick, Samuel. *The Path of Prayer,* 100.

[421] https://www.worldinvisible.com/library/wesley/8317/831711.htm

[422] Rogers, Adrian. "How to Pray for America," *Decision Magazine,* February 1, 2021.

[423] https://www.azquotes.com/quote/545436

[424] McConkey, James H. *Prayer. The Omnipotent Power of Prevailing Prayer.*

[425] https://www.preceptaustin.org/prayer_quotes, accessed June 15, 2022.

[426] Watt, Gordon B. *Effectual Fervent Prayer.* (London: Marshall, Morgan & Scott, 1927), 67.

[427] Melanchthon, Philip. *Dictionary of Burning Words of Brilliant Writers.* (1895), 466.

[428] Pearson, A. T. *The New Acts of the Apostles.*

[429] Spurgeon, C. H. "A Poor Man's Cry, and What Came of It," Sermon delivered March 8, 1891.

[430] Rogers, Adrian. "Did You Know You Have Authority over Satan?" *Love Worth Finding,* Daily Devotional, November 22, 2019.

[431] https://www.azquotes.com/quote/550387, accessed June 26, 2022.

[432] Spurgeon, C. H. *Sermons on Prayer.* "Opening the Mouth" (London: Marshall, Morgan, & Scott, 1962), 99.

[433] https://www.embounds.online/prayer-quotes

[434] Cowman, L. B. *Streams in the Desert.* (Grand Rapids: Zondervan, 1997), July 27.

[435] https://www.preceptaustin.org/prayer_quotes_devotionals_ illustrations, accessed August 15, 2022.

[436] Bounds, E. M. *The Possibilities of Prayer.* (CreateSpace Independent Publishing Platform, January 30, 2018), 27.

[437] Spurgeon, C. H. "Divine Surprises," Sermon delivered May 16, 1880.

[438] Exell, J. S. *The Biblical Illustrator: St. Luke* (Vol. III), "Theological Sketchbook." (London: Francis Griffiths, 1904), 337.

[439] MacArthur, John. "The Priority of Prayer" (sermon), November 25, 1979. https://www.gty.org/library/sermons-library/2235/the-priority-of-prayer, accessed June 8, 2022.

[440] Murray, Andrew. *With Christ in the School of Prayer,* 4.

[441] Spurgeon, C. H. *Morning and Evening.* (London: Passmore & Alabaster), May 19 (Morning).

[442] https://parade.com/1311380/kelseypelzer/prayer-quotes/, accessed May 30, 2022.

[443] Linton, John. *Great Preaching on Prayer.* (Murfreesboro, TN: Sword of the Lord Publishers, 1988), 163–168. The points stated are adapted from the sermon, "Unanswered Prayer"

[444] https://www.preceptaustin.org/prayer_quotes, accessed June 15, 2022.

[445] Spurgeon, C. H. *Morning and Evening,* March 29 (Evening).

[446] Laurie, Greg. "Waiting For Answers" (Devotion). March 3, 2014. https://harvest.org/resources/devotion/waiting-for-answers/, accessed June 28,2022.

[447] https://www.preceptaustin.org/prayer_quotes, accessed June 15, 2022.

[448] Moody, D. L. *Prevailing Prayer: What Hinders It?* (1884), 87.

[449] *Matthew Henry's Concise Commentary,* 2 Corinthians 12:9.

[450] Chadwick, Samuel. The Path to Prayer, 1931.

[451] Rogers, Adrian. *Adrian Rogers' Daily Devotionals.* "Your Infirmity May Reveal God's Glory," April 13.

[452] Henry, M. *Matthew Henry's Commentary on the Whole Bible: Complete and Unabridged in One Volume.* (Peabody: Hendrickson, 1994), 837.

[453] Spurgeon, C. H. *The Treasury of David: Psalms 56–87* (Vol. 3). (London; Edinburgh; New York: Marshall Brothers, n.d.), 114.

[454] Spurgeon, C. H. *Morning and Evening,* May 19.

[455] Parsons, Charles R. *An Hour with George Müller: The Man of Faith to Whom God Gave Millions.* (Interview with Müller at the close of his life).

[456] Chadwick, Samuel. *Path to Prayer.* (1931), Chapter 11.

[457] Hutson, Curtis, Ed. *Great Preaching on Prayer.* (Murfreesboro, TN: Sword of the Lord Publishers, 1988), 235.

[458] Spurgeon, C. H. "Boldness at the Throne." Sermon delivered September 14, 1873 at the Metropolitan Tabernacle.

[459] https://www.thegospelcoalition.org/article/9-things-you-should-know-about-prayer-in-the-bible1/

[460] Bounds, E. M. cited in *How to Live a Life of Prayer,* 112.

[461] Burns, James. *The Laws of Revival.* (Minneapolis: World Wide Productions, 1993), 33.

[462] Chadwick, Samuel (a friend of A. T. Pierson. *Path to Prayer.* (1931), Chapter 11.

[463] Finn, Nathan. "The Hundred-Year Prayer Meeting", June 1, 2022. https://www.desiringgod.org/articles/the-hundred-year-prayer-meeting, accessed December 10, 2022.

[464] Ibid.

[465] Spurgeon, C. H. "A Poor Man's Cry, and What Came of It," Sermon delivered March 8, 1891.

[466] Spurgeon, C. H. *Autobiography.* Volume 2: "The Full Harvest 1860–1892. (Edinburgh: The Banner of Truth Trust, 1973), 162.

[467] Ibid., 161.

[468] Ibid., 161–164.

[469] Spurgeon, C. H. "Behold, He Prayeth," Sermon delivered September 20, 1885.

[470] Redpath, Alan. *Victorious Christian Service.* (Old Tappan, NJ: Fleming H. Revell Company, 1958), 75.

[471] Ibid., 24.

[472] https://www.embounds.online/prayer-quotes, accessed June 23, 2022.

[473] https://www.preceptaustin.org/prayer_quotes, accessed June 15, 2022.

[474] Bounds, E. M. *The Necessity of Prayer.* (New York: Revell, 1929), Chapter 6.

[475] https://prayer-coach.com/prayer-quotes-e-m-bounds/, accessed June 17, 2022.

[476] Parker, Joseph. *The City Temple Pulpit: Sermons.* (London: Hodder and Stoughton, 1899), 173.

[477] Ryle, J. C. *A Call to Prayer.* (Grand Rapids, MI: Baker Book House, 1979), 35.

[478] Exell, J. S. *The Biblical Illustrator: St. Luke* (Vol. III), "Essex Remembrancer." (London: Francis Griffiths, 1904), 337.

[479] https://www.dailychristianquote.com/tag/persecution/, accessed February 5, 2021.

[480] https://www.christianquotes.info/quotes-by-topic/quotes-about-persecution/. Accessed February 17, 2021.

[481] Coleman, Robert E. *The Master Plan of Evangelism.* (Grand Rapids: Revell, 1993),94.

[482] Bounds, E. M. *The Essentials of Prayer: Prayer and Missions.* (Dallas: Gideon House Books, 2016), Chapter 13.

[483] Murray, Andrew. *With Christ in the School of Prayer.* (New York: Regal), 47.

[484] Hallesby, Ole. *Prayer.* (Minneapolis, Minnesota: Augsburg Publishing House, 1931), 35.

[485] https://www.azquotes.com/quote/1062319, accessed August 15, 2022.

[486] http://articles.ochristian.com/article2637.shtml

[487] https://bible.org/illustration/visitation-god

[488] https://pray4revival.com/

[489] https://dustincgeorge.com/2019/08/26/the-necessity-of-prayer/

[490] https://www.azquotes.com/quote/544810

[491] https://harvest.org/resources/devotion/a-prescription-for-revival/

[492] Smith, Shelton. Ed. *Great Preaching on Revival.* (Murfreesboro, TN: Sword of the Lord Publishers, 1997), 161.

[493] Spence-Jones, H. D. M. (Ed.). *Habakkuk.* (London; New York: Funk & Wagnalls Company, 1909), 57.

[494] Brengle, Samuel Logan. *Take Time to Be Holy: 365 Daily Inspirations to Bring You Closer to God.* (Tyndale House Publishers, Inc., 2013), 186.

[495] Murray, Andrew. *The Secret of Believing Prayer,* Chapter 12.

[496] https://gracequotes.org/author-quote/oswald-sanders/

[497] Spurgeon, C. H. "A Prayer for Revival," a Sermon delivered August 14, 1887.

[498] Ibid.

[499] https://www.goodreads.com/quotes/322408-our-praying-needs-to-be-pressed-and-pursued-with-an, accessed September 5, 2021.

[500] Dixon, A. C. Cited from John Piper. *Brothers, We Are Not Professionals,* 71.

[501] Spence-Jones, H. D. M. (Ed.). *Habakkuk.* (London; New York: Funk & Wagnalls Company, 1909), 63.

[502] Criswell, W. A. "Divine Healing," (Sermon). James 5:14–15. July 25, 1965. https:// wacriswell.com/sermons/1965/divine-healing-2/, accessed July 20, 2020.

[503] Swindoll, Chuck. "James: Hands-On Christianity, Suffering, Sickness, Sin—and Healing." https://insightforliving.swncdn.com/pdf/broadcast/2017.01.11-notes.pdf, accessed July 20, 2020.

[504] Criswell, W. A. "Divine Healing," (Sermon). James 5:14–15. July 25, 1965. https:// wacriswell.com/sermons/1965/divine-healing-2/, accessed July 20, 2020.

[505] https://www.forbes.com/quotes/author/alexis-carrel/, accessed June 29, 2022.

[506] Wiersbe, Warren, Compiler. *The Best of A. W. Tozer.* (Camp Hill, PA: Christian Publications, Inc., 1986), 62.

[507] https://www.preceptaustin.org/prayer_quotes, accessed June 25, 2022.

508 Criswell, W. A. "Divine Healing," (Sermon). James 5:14–15. July 25, 1965. https:// wacriswell.com/sermons/1965/divine-healing-2/, accessed July 20, 2020.

509 Adams, Jamie M. "Praying for Healing," (Article). https://www.nelsonprice.com/ praying-for-healing/, accessed July 21, 2020.

510 Lucado, Max. Tweet. Aug 4, 2016.

511 Storms, Samuel. *Healing and Holiness,* 10-11.

512 https://greenwichpres.org/mt-content/uploads/2021/03/prayer-for-healing_6046ae7852eee.pdf, accessed June 20, 2022.

513 https://www.preceptaustin.org/prayer_quotes, accessed June 15, 2022.

514 Chafer, Lewis. *True Evangelism,* Chapter 5.

515 Brengle, Samuel Logan. *Take Time to Be Holy: 365 Daily Inspirations to Bring You Closer to God.* (Tyndale House Publishers, Inc., 2013), 186.

516 Rice, John R. *The Soul-Winner's Fire.* (Murfreesboro: Sword of the Lord, 1941), 11.

517 https://www.azquotes.com/quote/544758

518 Rice, John R. *The Soul-Winner's Fire.* (Murfreesboro: Sword of the Lord, 1941), 11.

519 Wilkerson, David. *Bring Your Loved Ones to Christ.* (New Jersey: Fleming Revell Company, 1979), 116–117.

520 Sanders, J. Oswald. *The Divine Art of Soul Winning,* 40–41.

521 Hallesby, Ole. *Prayer.* (Minneapolis, Minnesota: Augsburg Publishing House, 1931), 87–88.

522 Spurgeon, C. H. *2,200 Quotations: From the Writings of Charles H. Spurgeon: Arranged Topically or Textually and Indexed by Subject, Scripture, and People,* (T. Carter, Ed.). (Grand Rapids, MI: Baker Books, 1995), 152.

523 Bounds, E. M. *A Treasury of Prayer.* (Racine, WI: BroadStreet Publishing Group, 1989), 78. [Quote originally attributed to John Welch but later sources cite McCheyne.]

524 Spurgeon, C. H. *Only A Prayer Meeting.* (Great Britain: Christian Focus Publications, 2000), 171.

525 Spurgeon, C. H. "The Story of God's Mighty Acts," Sermon delivered July 17, 1859.

526 Exell, J. S. *The Biblical Illustrator: Ephesians.* (New York; Chicago; Toronto; London; Edinburgh: Fleming H. Revell Company, n.d.), 684.

527 https://www.goodreads.com/author/quotes/3317101, accessed June 27, 2022,

[528] Bounds, E. M. https://www.preceptaustin.org/prayer_quotes

[529] https://www.azquotes.com/quote/1307149, accessed July 25, 2022.

[530] https://djameskennedy.org/devotional-detail/20150225-a-checklist-for-your-prayer-life, accessed May 9, 2017.

[531] https://www.azquotes.com/quote/1390185

[532] https://www.christianquotes.info/quotes-by-topic/quotes-about-intercession/, accessed June 20,2022.

[533] Murray, Andrew. *Helps to Intercession,* Preface.

[534] Chadwick, Samuel. *Path to Prayer.* (1931), Chapter 14.

[535] Swindoll, Chuck. "Tender Words from a Mentor" (sermon).

[536] https://www.christianquotes.info/quotes-by-topic/quotes-about-intercession/, accessed June 17, 2022.

[537] https://www.azquotes.com/quotes/topics/intercessory-prayer.html, accessed May 24, 2022.

[538] Duwel, Wesley. *Touch the World through Prayer.* (Grand Rapids: Zondervan Publishing Company, 1986), 60.

[539] https://gracequotes.org/topic/evangelism-prayer/

[540] https://www.inspiringquotes.us/author/8177-f-b-meyer/about-prayer, accessed June 22, 2022.

[541] *The Kings Business.* (Los Angeles, California, January 1939), 33.

[542] Spurgeon, C. H. "How to Keep the Heart," Sermon delivered February 21, 1858, New Park Chapel.

[543] https://www.preceptaustin.org/prayer_quotes, accessed June 24, 2022.

[544] Cited in I. D. E. Thomas. *A Puritan Golden Treasury.* (Edinburgh: Banner of Truth, 1977), 192.

[545] Bounds, E. M. *Preacher and Prayer.*

[546] McConkey, James. *The Three-Fold Secret of the Holy Spirit.* (Pittsburgh, PA: Silver Publishing Co., 1975), 102–103.

[547] *Preaching for God's Glory,* (Crossway, 1999), 43.

[548] *Preaching: Its Ideals and Inner Life,* (American Baptist Publication, 1990), 170.

[549] https://ccel.org/ccel/bounds/power/power.I_1.html

[550] *Lectures to My Students.* Lesson 3: The Preacher's Private Prayer.

[551] Ironside, H. A. *Praying in the Holy Spirit.* (Loizeaux Brothers), 59.

[552] Sorenson, *The Pulpit and the Pew.*

[553] Horne, G. *A Commentary on the Book of Psalms.* (New York: Robert Carter & Brothers,1856), 297.

[554] Hyman, Hon. Michael B. *Bench & Bar*, June 2016, vol. 46, no. 9.

[555] *Matthew Henry's Concise Bible Commentary,* Psalm 72:18–20.

[556] Henry, M. *Matthew Henry's Commentary on the Whole Bible: Complete and Unabridged in One Volume.* (Peabody: Hendrickson, 1994), 847.

[557] Spurgeon, C. H. *The Treasury of David: Psalms 56–87* (Vol. 3). (London; Edinburgh; New York: Marshall Brothers, n.d.), 232.

[558] Chadwick, Samuel. *The Path of Prayer,* (1931).

[559] MacKay, William Alexander. *Outpourings of the Spirit.* (Philadelphia: Presbyterian Board of Publication and Sabbath School Work, 1890), 136. [Good biographical sketches of great revivalists, chapter 9, pp. 114–124.]

[560] Ibid.

[561] Spurgeon, C. H. *Flowers from a Puritan's Garden.* (New York: Funk & Wagnalls, 1883).

[562] https://www.allchristianquotes.org/quotes/John_Bunyan/1655/, accessed July 30, 2022.